T0340234

ROUTLEDGE LIBRARY EDITIONS: HUMAN RESOURCE MANAGEMENT

Volume 18

TRAINING AT WORK

TRAINING AT WORK
A Critical Analysis of Policy and Practice

JEFF HYMAN

Routledge
Taylor & Francis Group

LONDON AND NEW YORK

First published in 1992 by Routledge

This edition first published in 2017
by Routledge
2 Park Square, Milton Park, Abingdon, Oxon OX14 4RN

and by Routledge
711 Third Avenue, New York, NY 10017

Routledge is an imprint of the Taylor & Francis Group, an informa business

© 1992 Jeff Hyman

All rights reserved. No part of this book may be reprinted or reproduced or utilised in any form or by any electronic, mechanical, or other means, now known or hereafter invented, including photocopying and recording, or in any information storage or retrieval system, without permission in writing from the publishers.

Trademark notice: Product or corporate names may be trademarks or registered trademarks, and are used only for identification and explanation without intent to infringe.

British Library Cataloguing in Publication Data
A catalogue record for this book is available from the British Library

ISBN: 978-1-138-80870-6 (Set)
ISBN: 978-1-315-18006-9 (Set) (ebk)
ISBN: 978-1-138-71503-5 (Volume 18) (hbk)
ISBN: 978-0-415-37691-4 (Volume 18) (pbk)
ISBN: 978-1-315-23107-5 (Volume 18) (ebk)

Publisher's Note
The publisher has gone to great lengths to ensure the quality of this reprint but points out that some imperfections in the original copies may be apparent.

Disclaimer
The publisher has made every effort to trace copyright holders and would welcome correspondence from those they have been unable to trace.

Training at work

A critical analysis of policy
and practice

Jeff Hyman

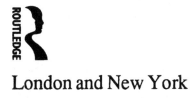

London and New York

First published 1992
by Routledge
11 New Fetter Lane, London EC4P 4EE

Simultaneously published in the USA and Canada
by Routledge
a division of Routledge, Chapman and Hall, Inc.
29 West 35th Street, New York, NY 10001

© 1992 Jeff Hyman

Typeset by LaserScript, Mitcham, Surrey
Printed and bound in Great Britain by
Mackays of Chatham PLC, Chatham, Kent

All rights reserved. No part of this book may be reprinted or reproduced or
utilized in any form or by any electronic, mechanical or other means, now
known or hereafter invented, including photocopying and recording, or in any
information storage or retrieval system, without permission in writing from
the publishers.

British Library Cataloguing in Publication Data

Hyman, J. D. (Jeffrey David)
   Training at Work
   I. Title
   658.3124

ISBN 0–415–05343–9

Library of Congress Cataloging in Publication Data

   Hyman, Jeff, 1945–
   Training at work: A critical analysis of policy and practice/Jeff Hyman
   Includes bibliographical references and index
   ISBN 0–415–05343–9
   1 Employees – Training of   I Title
HF5549.5.T7H95   1992
658.3'124–dc20

To my parents

Contents

Figures

Tables

Foreword

At the time of writing, the British economy is again facing the onset of a devastating recession. Business confidence is draining away as the rate of company failures accelerates. Investment in plant, machinery and people continues to fall and unemployment is growing at an almost unprecedented rate.

There are few signs of spring sunshine to dispel winter's gloom; employers are unable to find or have been unprepared to develop the skills which they require in order to survive; young people are striving to participate in a workforce which they are poorly equipped to enter; rising ranks of unemployed people are devoid of the qualities called for by employers desperate for skilled labour.

Employers are being pulled in different directions. Market disciplines encourage them to become lean and efficient, to keep costs low; and yet to survive companies must attract, motivate, retain and develop labour within this restrictive framework. Further, to relieve the chronic shortages of skilled manpower found throughout the country, the government has turned to hard-pressed employers as the chosen instrument for upgrading the national skills profile. Relying upon labour market liberalisation, the government has created new employer domi-nated bodies to co-ordinate the supply of labour with the demands for it, encouraged employer involvement in education and exhorted individual employers to train their staff. As a complementary strand tied to this market-driven approach, government controls on training provision have been relaxed whilst state expenditures on education and training have been subjected to tight and continuing scrutiny.

An examination of the ways in which employers have responded to the invitation to reconstruct the skills profile of the economy provides the main aim of this book, leading to a broader assessment of the efficacy of a market-driven training policy as a platform from which to launch the much-heralded 'skills revolution'.

Employer approaches to work-based training were evaluated in an in-depth survey conducted among private sector companies based in Scotland. Through comparisons with earlier studies undertaken in the 1980s it has been possible to assess the ways in which skill problems have been confronted during the market-driven decade of the 1980s. The results offer little evidence of 'revolutionary' change, suggesting that unless a major reformulation of priorities and policies is undertaken, the prognosis for Britain's future economic prospects looks bleak. The book concludes with a consideration of the directions which an alternative, more interventionist strategy might take.

In writing this book, I have become only too aware of the debt which is owed to the many institutions, colleagues and friends who have contributed to its development. The survey was only made possible with a grant from the University of Strathclyde Research and Development Fund, to whom I would like to record my appreciation. Without the responses of the companies who took time and trouble to complete a detailed and lengthy questionnaire, there would be no data on which to undertake the assessment. I am also indebted to Karen Bell, researcher to the project, who undertook much of the early survey analysis and whose proposed participation in the book was prevented by family and work commitments. Retyping the text from shaky word processor to finished manuscript was undertaken by Debbie Campbell from amidst a mass of other departmental commitments. Without her help, completion on time would have been impossible.

Sincere gratitude is offered to all friends and colleagues who have freely provided so much support over the past year in commenting upon drafts, in discussion over the subject and in much needed encouragement. Naming everyone would be impossible, but special thanks are owed to Pam Arksey, Chris Baldry and Heather Baldry, John MacInnes, Harvie Ramsay and Mairi Steele. Finally, for both her professional help and partnership, I owe more than thanks to Sabine Citron.

Jeff Hyman
University of Strathclyde
February 1991

Abbreviations

BGT	Business Growth Training
CBI	Confederation of British Industry
CMED	Council for Management Education and Development
CTC	City technology college
EDAP	Employee Development and Assistance Programme
ESC	Education Standards Council
ET	Employment Training
GCSE	General Certificate of Education
HRM	Human resource management
IDS	Income Data Services
IPM	Institute of Personnel Management
ITBs	Industry Training Boards
ITD	Institute of Training and Development
LEA	Local Education Authority
LEC	Local Enterprise Company
LJPC	Local Joint Programme Committee
MSC	Manpower Services Commission
NCVQ	National Council for Vocational Qualifications
NIESR	National Institute of Economic and Social Research
NTI	New Training Initiative
TA	Training Agency
TEC	Training and Enterprise Council
TGWU	Transport and General Workers Union
TVEI	Technical and Vocational Education Initiative
TUC	Trades Union Congress
VET	Vocational Education and Training
WIRS	Workplace Industrial Relations Survey
YT	Youth Training
YTS	Youth Training Scheme

Introduction

Many employers are heavily committed to training, and . . . their
investment is rising . . . Employers are investing in skills not because
they are compelled to, but because they see the advantage to their
businesses of doing so.

> (Secretary of State for Employment,
> Letter to the *Guardian*, 15 December 1990)

Many employers are spending large sums of money on training, but
unfortunately there are employers who are spending nothing, or very
little.

> (Reply from Labour Party Employment
> Spokesperson, *Guardian*, 22 December 1990)

BACKGROUND

This book explores the connections between training and work, though
it concentrates on the relationship between employers and training
provision. In particular, we want to ask whether people are now being
trained at and for work, or not trained, which has been for many years
the routine workplace experience of most employees in Britain.

Given that observers tend to agree upon the existence of a positive
relationship between training and the productive potential of workers
and managers, the lack of attention given to training in Britain throughout the years may be surprising, especially as improving work performance provides the springboard for economic development, the benefits
of which filter directly to all citizens through their standards of living.
On a wider scale, economic growth offers considerable political
potential, as illustrated by the remarks of a senior member of the Labour
Party:

Probably the single most important determinant of the way people vote is their perception of their living standards. If they see them rising steadily and feel better off, they will generally give a vote of satisfaction with the government. But if they feel them slipping or even merely stagnant, they will tend to be hostile.

(M. Meacher, *Guardian*, 22 January 1990)

The connections between the economic comfort of individuals, industrial competitiveness and the political process should ensure that governments take an active interest in trying to sustain an acceptable level of economic growth and, by extension, attempt to stimulate the productivity of industry, which is usually translated into trying to enhance the productive efforts of the nation's workforce. Spurred on by an eager media network, productivity growth has become a virility symbol by which governments and public alike measure economic and hence political success.

We shall see that while governments, and likewise employers, have adopted a variety of approaches in order to address the work productivity issue in the UK, a common and constant theme may be discerned: economic policy has chiefly focused on restraining the costs of labour. The problem has been that apart from short-term improvements usually occurring under spectacular and atypical conditions (as when output expands following a severe recession), productivity has never responded well or consistently to this form of treatment. A stuttering growth rate submitted to a succession of short-term and often contradictory government remedies has been the result. The most clearcut manifestation of this policy failure has been expressed in the familiar cycles of 'stop-go' as governments alternate deflationary measures to cool down an over-heated economy with bursts of economic stimulation aimed at boosting growth and safeguarding employment.

One source of productivity growth which has suffered from comparative neglect in Britain is through education and training. Explanations for this treatment will be considered in Chapter 1 below but at this point it is sufficient to note that, with few honourable exceptions, for the greater part of this century, lack of qualifications and skills have permeated UK industry from the most junior employees to the ranks of senior executive positions. A deficiency of training has, in particular, been a depressing feature of small firms, that sector of the economy for which so much promise for future growth and employment is held.

While it is difficult to quantify the contributions made by education and training to economic development, there is little question that these factors exert a positive influence in their own right and in synergy with other factors, such as technology (see Gospel 1991). The value of this relationship appears to have been recognised and appreciated by governments and employers in competitor countries, who have rarely been as short-sighted in their educational and training endeavours as their British counterparts. This different perspective is reflected in economic performance, where the UK has been regularly outstripped in terms of investment, output and productivity.

With the realisation of the Single European Market in 1992 and with dramatic economic and political change occurring throughout Eastern Europe, the position for UK manufacturers will steadily deteriorate as Britain slips between the requirements of supplying cheap and relatively unsophisticated labour for mass production industries and the high skills demanded by advanced technology. Our workforce will not be 'cheap' enough to compete with the former, nor sufficiently skilled to match the requirements of the latter, a fact well acknowledged, if somewhat belatedly, at government level: 'Do we as a nation compete in the high technology, high value added, high wage end of the spectrum? Or do we slide into a low technology, low value added, low wage economy' (Employment Secretary, M. Howard, reported in the *Guardian*, 9 February 1990).

The shift to a 'knowledge-based' industrial economy, itself contingent upon the development and application of technology, combined with the internationalisation and increasing sophistication of product and consumer markets and the heightened competition which these developments herald, all point to one conclusion which Britain must recognise: the neglect of training (and that of education for the majority of our population) must be reversed if rates and quality of production and economic advancement are to match those of our major trading partners. Attempts at unit cost reduction through attacking levels of pay (and the institutions established to protect the income and security of employees) have only succeeded in magnifying the problems of industrial decline yet have singularly failed to improve long-term productivity. As a response to complex economic developments, this approach can never succeed; it is simply the wrong remedy for the wrong illness.

Preference for minimising labour costs, rather than raising labour potential, is reflected in the analyses and policies of both governments and employers towards the workforce: personnel prescriptions are usually drawn up in terms of limiting rates of pay or in calling for restrictive changes in working practices and conditions. In this respect, productivity has assumed a key but narrow place in the consciousness of the three principal parties with a direct interest in the conduct of industrial relations. The government aims for higher productivity as a means to stimulate growth and to expand wealth. Employers have a direct interest in restraining labour costs in order to survive and compete both at home and internationally. Employees and their representative organisations, the trade unions, share in this interest as the direct recipients of the means adopted by employers to stimulate productivity growth; increased productivity associated with capital investment can mean higher pay, more opportunity and better living standards, though possibly with fewer workers. Employers' productivity drives could, alternatively, be manifested through intensifying employee effort along with low pay and little investment.

An underlying theme in this book is that productivity forms an inherent part of the processes of industrial relations, and as the 'front line' activity for organisational profitability or efficiency will always be so whilst there are people to organise and direct. The approaches adopted toward productivity growth will be examined below; what will become apparent is that whilst productivity enhancement, as it is usually defined, is an important contributor to organisational competitiveness, in itself it is not sufficient, for it is overall *performance* which provides the key to organisational effectiveness. It will also become apparent that training, one of the prime sources for performance growth, or 'performance productivity' as we shall call it, has been continually downplayed as part of the relations between the major interested parties. Governments have been reluctant to intervene formally in an area traditionally regarded as a matter for employers to determine according to their own market requirements. Employers, however, have seldom responded positively to this invitation to take responsibility for training. Employees, other than craft unions acting in protection of their skill boundaries, have also tended to react passively in their approach to training as an element of their dealings with employers.

Employment relations are conducted in the UK through a network involving State, employers and, to a significant extent, unions. Performance productivity looms large in the interests and activities of these parties and training can make a vital contribution to its enhancement. The logical outcome that stems from this system of industrial relationships is that training must assume higher priority for all three parties and that this priority and mutual interest can best be expressed through involvement by all major interested parties to training affairs at State level, both in policy-making and in the execution of these policies.

Such an approach would represent a significant departure from the mainstream of government thinking on training in this country, which by leaving training provision to be determined through independent 'voluntaristic' actions of individual employers or industries, has been largely absent in terms of a co-ordinated policy. As shall be seen, this emphasis on employer responsibility for training determination was strongly reaffirmed during the 'market relations' economic policy era of the 1980s. Our findings suggest that this approach has failed to raise the level and quality of training provision, pointing to the conclusion that market forces cannot be relied upon to satisfy the diverse training aspirations of State, employers and employees. Whilst market signals can guide aspects of policy, the short-term and hence potentially mis-leading nature of these signals would not be compatible with a longer-term planning process which British manpower policy lacks and needs. The competitive regulatory mechanisms assumed by the market also offer an explicit recognition of contrasting objectives between the parties, all of whom share an interest in expanding training provision, though with different perspectives over its funding and directions to be taken. This leads to the conclusion that training planning and associated activities are essentially a distributive process, best resolved through active pluralistic involvement by the major interested parties.

As training is of direct and immediate relevance to employers, em-ployees and their representatives, in order to complement centralised joint determination over the directions of training policy and its inte-gration with other labour market policies, the enterprise and workplace should provide the forum for training activity to be organised in terms of quantity, quality and monitoring, in line with nationally agreed policy guidelines.

The foundations for training provision are laid by the employer who decides on the nature of the product to be made or the service to be offered, the size, technological dimensions and siting of operations (which might, for example, be influenced by the availability of a reser-voir of relevant skills in the locality) and the calibre of staff necessary to undertake the tasks required in order to satisfy production requirements. Employers thus have a profound interest in training, or under appro-priate conditions in not training; if production technology is simple and relatively unchanging, if there is a ready supply of partially or fully trained labour from other sources, such as schools or other employers, if employers fear the loss of trained staff to competitors, or if they are apprehensive about costs associated with the training process or the potential for trained employees to demand improved terms and conditions, then employers may not display too much interest in training their employees.

If, however, employers are in need of skilled, adaptable and flexible labour as well as a stable or expanding workforce, they may train existing employees to meet their requirements and those of their customers. Even so, employers may prefer to keep their training programmes short in duration, informal in provision and specific to the workplace, thereby restricting opportunities for employees to mobilise their skills in search of better-rewarded work elsewhere or to make higher demands upon existing employers.

By contrast, employees might prefer training arrangements which extend opportunities for control over their existing or potential work environment. This is especially important in Britain, as employment conditions with the majority of employers are subject to the manifold insecurities which derive from a strong policy emphasis given to competitive product and labour market forces. They might want more say in decisions over who receives training and who provides the training. Arrangements preferred by employees might, for example, require sustained training programmes to be conducted at a distance from the immediate work environment and hence away from the control of work supervisors and, crucially, be capable of offering formal qualifications as transferable evidence for skill attainments.

The above arguments lead to the essential point that whilst employers and employees both stand to gain from training, they view the training process and training outcomes from different angles. We would contend that in common with other distributive aspects of their work relations, there are likely to be significant differences between the parties in terms of scope, direction, amount, formality[1] and expenditure preferences for training. In other words, training can be seen as an area of employment relations typified by a combination of convergent and divergent interests: convergent in the sense that training, like health and safety, is recognisable as being something which both employers and employees should aim to optimise, but divergent in that employer and employee interests in training provision are not identical. In this sense, training should be incorporated into work-based joint decision-making negotiating procedures where unions are recognised, or by other joint arrangements where they are not. These proposals are developed more fully in the concluding chapter.

THE STRUCTURE OF THE BOOK

This book is organised in two parts. The first section establishes the background against which employer training decisions and practice are set. Chapter 1 probes more deeply into the productivity debate and concludes that government and employer traditions of concentration on reduction of employment costs have not provided the correct key to unlock Britain's performance potential and are unlikely to do so in the future. The chapter posits that in a complex world, economic and organisational competitiveness can only be achieved by meeting wider performance criteria, which in turn emphasises the reasons for Britain's historical failure to train both employees and managers within a traditionally voluntaristic training and industrial relations framework.

As training is an implicit part of the employment relationship, which in turn is subject to State influence through industrial relations policy and legislation, Chapter 2 considers the role of the State with regard to employment relations in Britain with the main emphasis on current attempts at industrial relations reform as part of liberalising both the product market (notably in the public sector) and the labour market. Recognising the close links, or potential links, between education and training, the chapter also contemplates the changing educational scene in Britain, which for the past fifteen years has been subjected by government to an accelerating but fragmented vocational emphasis, with growing encouragement from the State for employer contributions to the educational process. The extent and effects of these changes and their implications for employer-sponsored training initiatives are examined. Educational weaknesses in terms of higher educational participation rates, neglect of engineering and technology and possible links with under-educated and poorly developed management in Britain are also scrutinised.

Chapter 3 extends the theme of examining national policy-making by turning to government efforts at manpower planning. Manpower policy can take place along a continuum extending from a highly interventionist role in planning for a country's manpower resources, to one in which it virtually abstains from involving itself other than acting as a signalling and informative service to labour market participants. During the 1980s, a traditionally non-interventionist approach by government was resumed and reinforced in Britain, following a relatively highly interventionist period in the 1960s, which was steadily diluted in the 1970s. For the historically high levels of workless young people and older unemployed, programmes have been introduced which rely heavily upon voluntary employer involvement. Additionally, and in order to augment this approach, remnants of older pluralist traditions, such as the tripartite involvement provided by the MSC, or joint bodies such as Training Boards, have progressively been eroded with the steady ascendence toward a market-dominated policy.

The final chapter in the first part of the book concludes with an examination of the traditions, policies and contexts for training adopted in other leading market economies. It also points out that whilst each country has adopted its own approach, each of them provides more education and more training more consistently than is or has been the case in Britain; these efforts are substantially reinforced by practical employer support for training by most of our trading partners.

Against this background of an openly market-dominated policy approach to training, and one which is designed to offer scope to employers to take diverse initiatives in the training field, the second part of the book examines employer practice with regard to training. Chapter 5 reviews key investigations conducted in Britain over the past decade, which collectively confirm a generally low organisational status for training activities; a cost-centred, rather than investment approach to the application of training; and organisations managed by poorly educated and under-developed executives.

Chapter 6 introduces the empirical work conducted by the author in summer 1989,[2] when 106 companies based in Scotland replied to an in-depth questionnaire about their training and personnel practices. This chapter concentrates on the backgrounds, qualifications and responsibilities of senior trainers in their organisations. The study found that only a minority of trainers were specialists in personnel and training matters and that most performed their training responsibilities among a range of other activities. Contrary to expectations, most training decisions were made at senior levels within organisations, but only in larger organisations was there evidence for personnel expertise inputs into these decisions.

Chapter 7 examines patterns of training expenditure in the survey companies and seeks evidence that firms are taking a more strategic perspective with regard to training. Though expenditure on training was said to have increased by the majority of respondents over the past year, and a majority anticipated further increases in the year ahead, overall stated expenditure was not high, varying from £73 per head annually in small concerns to £110 in companies with more than 500 employees. There were few signs that government-sponsored programmes for young trainees and especially long-term unemployed adults were being included as part of any strategic human resource planning system. Larger companies appear to be increasing their commitment to management development, but within limited budget constraints. Little evidence was found for formal involvement by employees in decision-making over training. Small firms offer little training to employees or to managers. These patterns emerged in an environment in which a substantial minority of survey companies were experiencing difficulties in recruiting skilled, managerial and technical staff.

The final two chapters draw upon the accumulated evidence to demonstrate the flimsiness of support for a market-based approach to resolve Britain's deep-seated skill weaknesses. This critique is followed in the concluding chapter by an appraisal of an alternative strategy, which attempts to put in place a more substantial training and vocational education framework in which governmental responsibility for overall co-ordination of these activities is openly endorsed. Recognising that State, employers and employees differ in their interests over training, the final chapter also proposes that the government should introduce mechanisms by which diverse interests over training may be confronted and reconciled in a constructive and forward-thinking manner.

Chapter 1

Britain's economic weakness

Productivity has never been higher.

> (Conservative Party radio broadcast, 1982,
> reported in Nichols 1986: 9)

The British economy is poised on the brink of recession, with output growth stagnating, unemployment in manufacturing set to rise and little sign of a rise in investment in the coming year.

> (CBI, reported in the *Financial Times*, 31 January 1990)

INTRODUCTION

It is widely acknowledged the Britain is failing to keep pace with the economic advances made by other countries (Cassels 1990: 14). A closely related worry has been (as the above quotes indicate) that economic growth has not occurred on a consistent basis; manufacturing industry experienced two decades of slow growth in the 1960s and 1970s followed by a considerable surge in the middle of the latter years of the 1980s, to be followed in turn by a dramatic slow-down in output growth in 1989 and 1990 (Ingram and Lindop 1990: 32–5; Blyton 1990). As suggested earlier, these failings carry considerable political as well as economic significance.

A number of explanations have been offered for Britain's poor and erratic economic performance, but the constant and dominant refrain has been to cast blame on the poor productivity of the nation's employed labour force. This chapter considers these alleged failings and suggests that productivity alone does not provide a reliable measure of economic effectiveness; broader aspects of performance need to be examined in terms of the quality of work, the effectiveness of management activities and managerial priorities in realising the potential of their assets through investment in capital and people.

PRODUCTIVITY OR PERFORMANCE?

Productivity can be defined as a ratio expressed between output (in the form of product or services) and inputs employed in order to achieve the output. The fewer the inputs used to produce a given output, the higher the level of productivity. Recognised inputs include the amount(s) of labour, capital and raw materials required as well as less tangible inputs such as standards of organisation and level of innovation (Owen Smith 1971: 6, 7).

One problem of measuring productivity is that less emphasis is placed on potential variability in some inputs than in others, possibly owing to the intangible nature of factors such as 'standards of organisation' and 'innovation'. As a consequence, productivity is usually, if not invariably, defined and measured in terms of 'output per man hour' (Owen Smith 1971: 6). However, serious consequences stem from this narrowing process; by using labour as the principal source of measurement, productivity variations, perhaps identified precariously through international comparison, are often attributed to deficiencies in the labour input. As potentially or technically the easiest or quickest of inputs to measure, this should come as no surprise. Owen Smith illustrates the focus on labour and the reactions of labour when he asserts that longer hours, more intensive work, better work organisation and capital substitution are the prime factors influencing productivity (1971: 11). Recent interest in increasing the flexibility of labour as a primary source of productivity growth offers a more contemporary interpretation of the same theme, especially when many flexibility trends include: extending the role of craft workers into 'less specialised elements of other trades . . . extending craft jobs to include less skilled work . . . extending the jobs of semi-skilled workers to include some basic maintenance work' (Ingram and Lindop 1990: 34).

Second, attention is not only primarily focused on labour but, as the prime influences noted above demonstrate, specifically on levels of *effort* by concentrating on time worked and intensification of work. The reluctance of British engineering employers to reduce the length of the standard working week from its present 39 hours and their refusal to negotiate the reorganisation of work to fit into a shorter working week helps demonstrate how deeply embedded is this concept of time worked as a contributor to productivity. The emphasis on level of output also illustrates a further problem in examining productivity in effort-related terms; the *quality* of output and its contributory labour inputs is in risk of neglect.

Relying upon effort and output as the major productivity variables can point to serious consequences in pursuing organisational objectives, which might be downgraded in search of accessibly cheap markets rather than face quality-based competition. In the developed world, however, products and services are not purchased merely or even principally on the basis of price; quality, value and reliability are increasingly promoted as the prime features of product or services provision. Under these conditions, to measure productivity in terms of effort and of output becomes both meaningless and harmful. It is meaningless because unless measurement and evaluation criteria expand and deepen beyond the narrow limits imposed by assessing an effort–output relationship, then organisational competitiveness can suffer. An obvious example of the meaninglessness of these variables is provided by the service sector, where output and effort could both be seen as elusive targets for attainment. For this reason, productivity measurements are invariably conducted in manufacturing industry. Even in manufacturing, relying upon these criteria can have damaging effects, because productivity measurement risks neglecting vital quality-based contributors to organisational growth or even survival.

Emphasis on labour effort also helps to deflect attention from the responsibilities of management. We shall see later that in its treatment of training and development, management has shown commendable consistency in its neglect of training provision among its own ranks. It is recognised by many contemporary observers of the management scene that performance productivity weaknesses are attributable in a considerable measure to the performance capabilities of British managers.

It would seem that the limitations of emphasising worker output as the main focus for productivity measurement are beginning to have some effect in industry. In particular, two trends are slowly, and perhaps uncertainly, beginning to emerge. First, attempts at assessing attainments of organisational objectives in terms of performance are increasing. Second, performance pertains to the entire organisation, to all employees, rather than being confined to a narrow focus on the labour of manual workers. Concentrating upon performance can also be undertaken in service industries in both public and private sectors.

It is possible that a coalition of factors is currently leading management toward the adoption of a widening range of assessment criteria based upon principles of target setting, performance monitoring and associating rewards with performance achievement. Performance appraisal is acknowledged to have increased in coverage, both in terms of the expanding number of organisations which use the technique and also by extending the range of occupations concerned to include non-managerial employees (Long 1986). Appraisal has also changed in approach from a generally indeterminate 'trait-based' system to one in which individual performance is matched against behavioural and measurable task-based criteria. The incidence of performance-related pay, typically based upon techniques of appraisal, is also generally held to have increased over the past few years (see, for example, Fowler 1988; Kinnie and Lowe 1990).

An example of changed emphasis is provided by recent interest in the concept of 'performance management', a relatively new approach which reflects and embraces these broader performance concerns of management by translating organisational objectives, policies and priorities into individual accountabilities, goals and plans.

A recent practitioner guide, published by a local authority, demon-strates how these aims might be achieved in operation through the introduction of five tiers of management practice geared to 'monitor the effectiveness of organisation'. The performance relationship is openly stated through:

1 Function and target setting, which identifies main areas of activity and the ways in which individuals contribute to them.
2 Pyramid performance monitoring, involving performance assess-ment at all levels, based upon identifying 'key tasks' at each level.
3 Structure and communication geared to 'discuss progress, solve operational problems and develop group awareness' at the lower level and 'concentrate . . . on performance trends, policy and direction' at more senior management levels.
4 Staff development and appraisal, to be established on a systematic basis and conducted regularly.
5 Management Information Systems, to facilitate performance measurement against pre-set targets.

(Royal Borough of Windsor and Maidenhead 1986)

Several implications arise from this shift in emphasis from effort-linked to broader-based performance productivity. It indicates that systems of management control in terms of remuneration policy, discipline and areas of responsibility are all likely to come under growing managerial scrutiny. In particular, we see that a change of this nature puts far more emphasis upon the management of the employment relationship, as reflected in the much discussed shift toward a 'human resource' centred approach of employee relations, which purports to treat employees as organisational assets whose potential for contribution to the organisation is shaped and developed through regular and systematic interaction with management.

Most crucially, emphasis on performance highlights the importance of training and development of staff. Part of the rationale for performance appraisal is to identify weaknesses correctable through training as well as to illuminate employee potential for enhancement, to develop performance rather than to assess and comment upon it (Randell 1989: 161). Individuals can expect to realise their optimal performance-related pay levels by achieving established (and frequently mutually agreed in advance) targets and are consequently likely to welcome or insist upon training opportunities which assist them to meet their targets and objectives. Similarly, the performance management approach outlined above is unambiguously contingent upon continuous employee development for its operation and success.

An additional weakness might be overlooked by allocating responsibility for the growth of productivity to individual effort-related inputs. What is also important, though again difficult to specify, is the degree of integration or synergy exerted between different inputs. Advanced technology introduced by an authoritarian management to an unprepared workforce may have deleterious effects on performance as well as upon morale; bearing in mind our earlier points about the labour focus of productivity, in such circumstances it would be most likely that workforce 'shortcomings' would be identified as the source of emergent problems. And attributing responsibility in this way certainly has been the tradition in Britain. As mentioned above, the efforts of both governments and employers have concentrated on gaining employee and union compliance to initiatives designed to increase levels of effort or to reduce unit labour costs; invariably, these initiatives affect the terms and conditions of employees. Hesitation by employees, and particularly by their unions, to accept new and possibly adverse work arrangements can be interpreted as raising the costs of the input side of the productivity equation, either through directly blocking a clumsily introduced change or through increasing the cost of its implementation. The line of responsibility, from uncompetitive economic performance, to low productivity, to 'poor employee attitudes' and 'obstructive' unions can be all too readily, if inaccurately, traced.

Despite the emerging trends noted above, it will perhaps not come as too much of a surprise, therefore, that still the most common and persistent reason offered in explanation for Britain's flagging economic performance is that workers in Britain are not prepared to work as hard, as flexibly or as enthusiastically as their Continental, American or especially, Japanese counterparts (Nichols 1986). Shared and promoted by employers, public and to varying degrees by governments of all persuasions (Nichols 1986: 15–20), this popular and simple image has been enlarged, and frequently distorted, by a media and consultancy network only too eager to hold collective worker activity responsible for low productivity and, by extrapolation, for poor national economic performance.

With the source of Britain's economic ills pointed squarely, if not entirely fairly, at worker limitations, prescriptions as to remedies have unfailingly tended to rely on and gravitate toward the reform of industrial relations and, specifically, of union behaviour. As economic difficulties multiplied in the post-war years, successive governments attempted to apply their cures for what became known as the 'British disease', portrayed as demonstrations of worker intransigence, greed and resistance to change.

Consequently, from the 1960s onwards, governments grappled with multiple and complex problems of maintaining high levels of employment, restraining inflation and achieving a healthy balance of payments by attempting to shackle the bargaining influence of trade unions through incomes policies, restrictive legislation or both. Governments sympathetic to organised labour might attempt to move toward the same ends through different means, perhaps by endeavouring to secure formal union commitment to bargaining restrictions in exchange for involvement in economic and industrial policy-making and membership of prestigious government-sponsored bodies, such as the National Economic Development Council.

Hence, a recurring priority for government in their endeavours to reform union behaviour has been to concentrate on reductions in labour costs. Incomes policies which limit the growth of pay have been common features of government economic regulation. However, these policies have often expressly excluded 'self-financing' productivity deals in which workers agree to concede defensive practices in return for increased pay.

Legislation has been passed to encourage workers to accept job loss by offering statutory minimal payments for redundant skills. In practice, these minimal levels are often exceeded by agreements jointly negotiated between managements and unions or by superior redundancy terms offered by management alone. Employer emphasis on worker productivity has been further channelled through remuneration practice which aims to link elements of pay directly to output by the use of incentive bonuses and value-added pay schemes.

As we advance into the new decade it is becoming apparent that with insufficient attention paid to the wider factor inputs noted above, the problems of performance productivity have not been resolved through reliance upon labour cost reduction. As the relative inefficiency of British industry continues to dominate economic and political thinking it is unlikely that attempts to restrict labour costs will slacken. Conversely, we would expect that Britain's uncomfortably tight squeeze into the European Exchange Rate (ERM) mechanism will increase pressures on employers to maintain a tight rein on their costs. Whilst no-one would dispute that it is in an employer's best interests to maintain control over costs, if this overlaps into a neglect of longer-term investment needs, the implications for future prosperity would be serious. Evidence suggests that many employers in Britain continue to treat training expenditure specifically as a labour cost and under these conditions we can anticipate an intensification of the problems of the post-war years. Recent responses from employers to the disciplines imposed by ERM membership makes for all-too familiar and dismal reading:

> ECC International, the china clay producer . . . stopped taking on apprentices at a time when it is cutting 750 of its 5,000 workers. Last year 24 apprentices began training with the company. This year, there are none.
>
> *(Financial Times*, 3 December 1990)

The same article also highlights the vulnerability of both training budgets and personnel manager influence to cost considerations, points which will be taken up in greater depth in Chapters 6 and 7. Given a training budget at the start of the year, the personnel manager of a printing company has subsequently seen the sum peremptorily removed by senior management. His comments illuminate a pervasive occurrence in British industry when faced by economic downturn: 'Training has been slashed and we have not taken on any apprentices this year. Two years ago we had half a dozen' (*Financial Times*, 3 December 1990).

The failure of attempts to improve labour productivity through concentrating on reducing labour costs should not come as a surprise. In a broader context, workers do not readily embrace the reality of redundancy however 'generous' the payments, when alternative work is unlikely to be available, when transferable skills and the opportunities to apply them are lacking and when the existence of job loss procedures coupled with management readiness to use them provide stark confirmation and formalisation of the precarious security provided by the contractual employment relationship.

Indeed, we would contend that the bulk of reform measures taken by governments and employers which have been geared to lower the cost of labour, whether through reducing staffing levels (redundancy) or by restricting pay, contain inherent weaknesses; most importantly, insufficient attention has been placed upon increasing the *performance capability* of labour. Some contend that this developmental approach, too, has been resisted through union obstructions and could point to demarcation disputes, inflexibility and the difficulties management face in introducing change into work in the face of union resistance. Certainly in the past, a formidable obstacle to achieving greater flexibility has been the strength, organisational capability and determination of craft unions to protect their skills and status through the apprenticeship system (Sheldrake and Vickerstaffe 1987: 31). Equally though, there is little evidence to suggest that employers attempted to address the problem of security which lies at the heart of union resistance to management initiatives to change work practices.

A second weakness concerns the fact that whilst there is obvious validity in the argument that unions serve to protect the security and earnings of members and that this defensive role could restrict management actions by raising implementation costs of new work initiatives, this is by no means the whole story. For example, there is little documented evidence that unions oppose the introduction of new technology; in fact, the opposite seems to be the case (Daniel 1987: 263–7; McLoughlin and Clark 1988: 72–4, Fogarty and Brooks 1986: 9). Provided unions receive assurance that members will derive benefit or will not be materially disadvantaged, they readily embrace both the concept and practice of new technology. What does seem to be clear is that union participation in the decision-making process is an important feature for acceptability of the application of advances in technology. This point is clearly demonstrated by the TUC checklist on new technology agreements which emphasises change and monitoring by agreement, early union involvement in the decision-making machinery, and assurances of retraining, earnings protection and the priority of health and safety for operators (McLoughlin and Clark 1988: 76).

An additional reservation which causes us to cast doubt on the union resistance thesis concerns the performance of non-unionised companies. For these companies, Daniel's analysis of the Workplace Industrial Relations Survey showed a lower level of technological innovation than in equivalent unionised workplaces (Daniel 1987: 34). Even in the absence of unions, it seems that the establishment of effective communication and consultative mechanisms to secure the commitment of staff to proposed change is needed (McLoughlin and Clark 1988: 93). If obstruction by unions to the introduction of new technology is not as prevalent as the media stereotypes would suggest, we might need to turn to alternative or additional explanations for Britain's weak economic record.

THE FAILURE TO INVEST

A major and continuing contributor to the problems of the UK economy has been the inability, or unwillingness, of domestic manufacturers to compete with overseas producers. In the aftermath of the Second World War, a popular explanation was the disadvantage of coping with a relatively intact but obsolete industrial infrastructure, unlike the Germans and Japanese, who enjoyed the twin benefits of a 'fresh start' and assistance from occupying powers. As Fox points out, however, it was probably the continuation of 'traditional assumptions, values and institutions', supporting a resumed global responsibility for which the country was no longer equipped, which did more to subvert economic performance at this stage (Fox 1985: 363). This was especially unfortunate as resumption of this role demanded a continual drain on the country's research and development capability in order to support military expenditure and in the maintenance of a high overall defence expenditure to the neglect of helping to finance potential growth industries.

Further, it was seldom pointed out that other countries, and notably America, were able to sustain significantly higher rates of growth than the UK whilst also being denied the opportunity for fundamental reconstruction. Neither was the point elaborated that productivity in the United States had continuously exceeded that of Britain throughout the twentieth century, and often by a factor of two or more (Nichols 1986: 3). Equally worrying, assistance for reconstruction was indeed provided, such that in the early 1950s, a quarter of world manufactures was produced by Britain (Gamble 1981: 106) and decline has been most marked since that period.

Featured in Britain's long decline is, however, one undeniable and common strand; domestic manufacturers have not been prepared to invest in plant, machinery and technology to the same extent as our competitors. Again, responsibility for this could be, and often is, laid at the door of the conservatism of trade unions and the lack of direction they offer to British workers to adapt, learn new techniques, or accept changes in working practice. The above studies, however, indicate that at most, this can only provide a partial explanation.

Conversely, the limited horizons of shareholders whose interests in securing short-term profit at the expense of long-term growth combine with a predatory take-over climate to dissuade manufacturers from investment which might detract from short-term profitability. These deficiencies would be compounded by a domestic finance market, which, unlike many other market economies, has separated finance capital from manufacturing capital, leading to considerable pressure by the former on the latter to maintain short-term profitability. Uncertainty and fluctuations in government economic policy have provided another substantial barrier to capital investment.

Therefore, a potentially more important factor than the mythical 'mindless obstruction' of unions is to assess the extent to which employers are committed to stable and continuing investment programmes. Despite the clamour emanating from government officials, employer representative bodies and sections of the press that we continue 'to pay ourselves more than we earn' there is in fact little empirical support for such notions. Indeed, by international standards, pay levels in the UK are not high whilst low pay seems to be endemic (Pearson 1985).

Low rates of pay could well be a significant factor in industry's well-recognised reluctance to invest; cheap labour, relatively easily removed, may well serve as an alternative to irrevocable commitment to expensive and non-disposable capital investment from which long-term returns are required to secure the value of the investment; and as we have indicated, 'long-term' considerations have not especially attracted British industry in the past (Dore 1985).

THE FAILURE TO TRAIN

A point closely related to their failure to invest, which reinforces employer culpability for poor economic performance, has been their continual reluctance to train and develop employees. Until recent years, training was confined virtually exclusively to the craft occupations in the form of the time-served apprenticeship. According to Sheldrake and Vickerstaffe, this provided the mainstay of British training practice

(1987: 56). Craft unions would oppose moves by employer or government to extend training to wider sections of the working population, and
as these restrictions offered little discomfort to employers during the
post-war boom years, little attempt was made by them to address the
issue.

However, the defensive instincts of craft unions can provide only
partial explanation for employers' failure to train. As we argue above,
low pay has been an integral feature of UK employment life. Skilled
labour, particularly when associated with new and highly productive
technology is both expensive to train, easy to lose through 'poaching'
and hence, costly to maintain through offering higher pay, better
working conditions and more stimulating work. Highly skilled labour
arguably also requires to be associated with a more open and participative management style, a feature which has largely been conspicuous
by its absence in British management practice. The need for extensive
reform of employment practice which would be associated with a
training-centred approach could well deter employers from embarking
upon a route from which it would subsequently be difficult to disem-
bark. Hence, with the State largely absolving itself from responsibility
for occupational and workplace training there seems to be little pressure
or incentive for employers to train. Their preference for informality,
already well-established as a feature of employment relations (Sisson
and Brown 1983) would seem to extend equally to training practice.
This would allow employers to withdraw from training at short notice
(see above), and not be tied to fixed, or agreed, commitments with
employees or their representatives.

An additional constraint against developing a training ethos has been
a continuing tradition in British industrial life which emphasises the
value of experience as the main contributor to workplace competence.
Allied to possession of the right 'qualities' nowhere has this been more
evident than in the neglect of training, development and education for
managers. It is hard to blame the trade unions for this state of affairs;
until recently only small proportions of managerial staff in specific
industries have been union members, and with these unions often acting
as quasi-professions aiming to improve and develop occupational
standards, there would be little resistance to the provision of training
opportunities were these to be offered. The truth is that only in rare
instances have these opportunities been granted.

Again, we must return to the myopic time horizons and preference for
control through informality displayed by many British employers as an
explanation for training negligence. This tradition is reinforced by an

occupational personnel and training weakness in which the function has seldom enjoyed elevated status in managerial circles. According to the Workplace Industrial Relations Survey (WIRS) findings, in 1984 only about 43 per cent of establishments had Board of Director members with specialist personnel responsibilities (Millward and Stevens 1986: 34). Many personnel specialists serve, in Tyson and Fell's (1986) words, as administrative 'clerks of the works' or alternatively as 'contract managers' in maintaining peace and stability in unionised environments. The proportion of personnel specialists with strategic and developmental responsibilities is rather less, as confirmed by the WIRS study. A recent study shows that though two-thirds of organisations with more than 200 employees have a written corporate strategy, in only half of these was a senior human resource representative involved at the decision stage. Seven out of ten respondents confirmed that they had a personnel strategy, but in only 40 per cent of cases was this a formal written document. Other signs of personnel detachment from strategic concerns were that a third of human resource specialists were unable to specify their labour costs and 40 per cent did not know the proportion of labour costs allocated to training (Brewster and Smith 1990).

Even with a management sympathetic to personnel, a major difficulty for personnel and training managers has been to convince senior management of the potential value of the contribution to be made by these activities to organisational performance. This association between training and performance of course becomes more difficult to establish, the longer the time scale involved: hence, employee development is often neglected owing to the difficulties personnel face in placing investment value on its provision. Also, as we have seen above, as a further demonstration of short-term thinking, training is often the first activity to be cut with the first sign of economic downturn.

SUMMARY

Britain is facing fierce competitive pressures from ever widening sources. The Single European Market becomes established in 1992, competition from newly liberalised Eastern Europe and a united Germany will increase, and Pacific Rim countries are strengthening their efforts to expand their share of world trade. Among market economies, Britain remains weak and vulnerable.

Britain's weaknesses can be traced to a number of sources, of which poor productivity performance is a major factor. It is recognised, if harder to prove, that this poor performance is directly associated with the persistent failure of employers to train and develop their employees and managers.

It could, with justification, be asserted that training is not necessarily the sole responsibility of employers; that if there have been deficiencies, then these should be viewed through a wider perspective than that provided by employers alone. To this we would agree, but as employers owe responsibility to their shareholders, customers and employees to produce effectively for the present and for the future, then it is in the interests of employers to be certain that they are taking the steps necessary to ensure that these commitments are met. In this sense, training provision forms an essential part of employer commitment to their stakeholders.

Nevertheless, other sources have been cited as having some responsibility for preparing people for work and to help in adjusting the supply of labour to the demands of new working conditions. Principal among these is the government, through its manpower and education policy-making. The contemporary industrial relations and educational role of government is examined in Chapter 2, followed by a review of government-sponsored manpower policies in Chapter 3.

Chapter 2

The response of the State
Reforms of industrial relations and education

> Since 1979, the Government have helped create an economic climate in which the British economy can prosper and grow. Britain is now reaping the benefits.
>
> (Employment for the 1990s 1988: 3)

During the 1970s, Britain's accumulating economic distress was reflected in political uncertainty, punctuated at key points by genuine crises, as successive governments struggled to maintain economic stability. The Conservative government led by Edward Heath succumbed in 1974, followed in similar fashion by a Labour administration five years later. In both cases immediate crisis was precipitated by the failure to control public sector pay through the imposition of incomes policy. More fundamentally, the tensions inherent in maintaining a productive but stable economy through Keynesian intervention were becoming increasingly apparent as inflation soared against a background of growing unemployment and industrial disaffection.

With the election of Mrs Thatcher's Conservative administration in 1979 an economic and political change of direction became openly expressed in the commitment given by the government to revitalise economic performance through reliance upon market disciplines in preference to management of the mixed economy by the State.

A number of crucial strands in the government's programme since 1979 stand out as part of its radical attempt to reform economic behaviour. These strands weave into an ideological fabric which aimed to highlight the superior productive force of individualism, self-help and private enterprise (collectively represented as the 'enterprise culture'), at the expense of the discredited collectivist, welfare and public sector emphasis which had dominated post-war political thinking. The principal integrated instruments of change were directed toward liberalisation of supply-side labour inputs to economic activity, involving, respectively, reform of industrial relations, orientation of education toward vocationalism and the articulation of an active manpower policy through the private sector. These programmes were to be implemented against a background of deepening economic recession for which the control of inflation formed the overriding policy objective, dominating other economic performance criteria such as 'interest rates, exchange rates, output, employment or the balance of trade' (MacInnes 1987: 51). The priority given to controlling inflation meant that the reform programmes were also to be implemented within a framework of considerable financial constraint.

The main instrument used to launch this deflationary assault was control of the supply of money and the initial outcome was a severe and prolonged reduction in output accompanied by growing unemployment. Jobless levels rose from 1.2 million in 1979 to a peak of 3.1 million in 1986, representing an unemployment rate of 11.5 per cent of the total working population. In manufacturing alone, the shake-out was so severe that 1.5 million jobs, representing 20 per cent of the workforce, were lost between the years 1980 and 1982 (Cassels 1990: 20). A workforce of 7.5 million in 1973 had been reduced to little more than 5 million by 1987: from 35 per cent of the employed workforce in 1973 to 19 per cent in 1990 (Blyton 1990).

THE REFORM OF INDUSTRIAL RELATIONS

Trade unions, whose membership was concentrated in relatively unskilled work in traditional manufacturing industry, were especially vulnerable to the growth of unemployment; from a peak level of 13.2 million in 1979, membership slumped to under 10.6 million by 1988 (Employment for the 1990s 1988: 17). The biggest union catering for general workers, the TGWU, alone lost nearly three-quarters of a million members between 1979 and 1988. During the same period the government was putting its reform package into action with its main thrust aimed largely at tackling the perceived 'union problem' discussed in the previous chapter. Hence, monetarist policy was reinforced by a set of measures directed at removing obstacles to free-market pay determination. This was to be achieved primarily by curtailing union access to government-sponsored policy-making bodies, by reducing the scope and influence of the public sector where unions are well-represented numerically and by undermining union bargaining power in both public and private sectors.

Tackling and removing these inflexibilities, the country was informed, would provide the only ('There is no alternative') means to ensure future prosperity and growth. The leading edge of this programme was a stream of legislation intended to curb union organisation and bargaining activities. Restrictions on the closed shop, picketing and industrial action were tightened successively by a series of Acts appearing regularly throughout the 1980s. Union influence over pay determination was indirectly loosened through limiting the activities of Wages Councils, established to protect the earnings of employees in weakly organised industries. The scope of these Councils was first narrowed to exclude under-21-year-olds, and then recommended for abolition on the grounds that statutorily backed pay determination may exert inhibiting effects on employers' 'business developments on which job creation depends' (Employment for the 1990s 1988: 27). The long established convention that government contractors pay minimum negotiated rates for the industry was also removed. Individual employment rights were curtailed in those areas where it was believed they might conflict with the labour market freedoms of employers.

Reducing the size and influence of the public sector was to be achieved through the process of privatisation, involving the disposal of sections of publicly owned enterprises to the private sector for exposure to competitive forces. Legislation was passed requiring competitive tendering for certain services provided by public authorities in order to increase competition in those areas of the public domain not deemed suitable or ready for the government's privatisation programme. Efficiency was further encouraged through the imposition of cash limits on the budgets of publicly funded services or, where appropriate, by the removal of State-supported subsidies. Relieved of State and union restrictions, employers were expected and encouraged to exercise their new-found market freedoms in the pursuit of 'wealth creation' in the private sphere and by operating with greater efficiency in the public sector. In both cases, heavy emphasis was placed on reducing unit labour costs through restructuring pay determination and constraining union bargaining activities.

The government's market orientation has been supplemented by a less interventionist strand of policy designed to enhance labour competitiveness or flexibility in the private sector, through offering tax concessions to employers to encourage the adoption of payment systems which recognise and reward employee contributions to increased profitability. Two main approaches have received this tax-favourable treatment: share schemes for employees, which intend to promote an 'enterprise' ethic through linking individual responsibility and reward with the benefits of property ownership, and profit-related pay, where a portion of employee pay varies directly with profitability.

Employer reaction to these two approaches had differed. Whilst taking advantage of various share scheme facilities in significant numbers and coverage (about 2 million employees are now able to participate in government-approved share schemes, see IDS 1990) the response by employers to profit-linked pay has been mixed with only a 1,000 live schemes covering under a quarter of a million employees operating three years after government approval was granted: indeed, many management sympathisers opposed to governmental attempts to exercise influence in employer remuneration practices have openly rejected this approach to pay flexibility (IPM 1986). Share schemes and profit-related pay do share one common characteristic; they are promoted on grounds of uniform applicability to all employees, management and their subordinates alike. Some commentators see this approach as offering tangible rewards in terms of common identity and increased productivity, whilst others are less convinced of these links (see Bell and Hanson 1987; Estrin and Wadhwani 1986).

Labour market flexibility has also been promoted through the support offered by the government to self-employment and to small firms formation (see Chapter 7). It has been suggested that there are currently 750,000 independent businesses with fewer than 50 employees. Of these, more than one-third had been established in the years 1982–8 (Hakim 1989: 32–4). Self-employment grew by 60 per cent between 1980 and 1988 (Mayes and Moir 1989: 15).

Notwithstanding these exhortative initiatives, the bulk of the government attention for productivity improvement has been directed at 'correcting' the behaviour of trade unions by the range of approaches outlined above, coupled with continuing rhetoric about the need not to 'pay ourselves more than we can afford'. In other words, the wide-ranging reforms introduced by the government have maintained the traditional emphasis of linking poor performance of the UK economy with union behaviour and conservatism, despite accumulating evidence, from the seminal Donovan Report onwards (1968: paras 303–4), that other factors contribute to this record. The strength of the approach may have intensified, but the directions have scarcely varied at all. And following a decade of progressively restrictive legislation and barely disguised opposition to collectivist employment relations, deployed at a time when union influence has been severely curtailed through unemployment, industrial restructuring and technological change, the government continues to heap blame on union attitudes and behaviour for shortcomings in economic performance (Employment for the 1990s 1988: 17).

The consequences of these governmental initiatives have been diverse: first, there has been a reduction in public sector employment in areas such as the civil service and industries transferred to the private sector. Second, structural shifts from traditional manufacturing to smaller unit high technology and service sector operations have accompanied high levels of unemployment, competitive pressures for products and services, and a diminution in industrial action by trade unions. Third, levels of union membership, itself a good barometer of industrial relations activity, suffered during the decade, declining from a density of 54.1 per cent in 1979 to 43.0 per cent by 1985 (Kelly 1988: 261).

An early cause and consequence of this reordering was the stasis in production. From a low output and high unemployment base, productivity however did begin to show dramatic improvement, averaging 5.2 per cent annual growth in manufacturing for the years 1980–8, compared with 1.6 per cent annually for the previous decade. Whether this improvement was attributable to government industrial relations policy resulting in more efficient working, or primarily a consequence of output expanded from a low base line using a much depleted labour force is still under dispute (see Brittan 1990). What has become apparent is that many of the productivity gains of the early 1980s have been subsequently eroded as lack of innovation and low skills, compounded by inflation and uncertainty in the Government's economic policies have conspired to prevent manufacturing penetration into high-quality domestic and export markets (Gapper 1990; *Financial Times*, 23 January 1990, 17 March 1990; Cassels 1990: 19).

Bearing in mind our earlier points concerning the overall lack of opposition by unions to technological or workplace change, the developments described above might be expected to provide an appropriate context for employers to restructure work practices and arrangements in preparing their workforces for the challenges of the 1990s. Nevertheless, the government also considered that the structural shifts in industry, high and persisting levels of youth and regional unemployment should be supplemented with broader 'supply side' initiatives to reinforce the industrial relations reorientation toward a less welfare-oriented, more individualistic self-help enterprise culture. An obvious target was education, which increasingly since the 1970s had been accused not merely of being out of touch with the needs of an advanced technological economy, but of possessing values inimicable to its progress.

THE REFORM OF EDUCATION

What is the purpose of education? The question is frequently posed in different ways by children, parents, teachers, providers such as education authorities under local political control, employers and politicians. Philosophers, sociologists, economists and psychologists and many others with a concerned interest also contribute to the debate. It might be more appropriate perhaps, to restate the questions in plural form, for it appears that there are a number of possible purposes to which education can be directed, co-existing but competing in uneasy tension. Under such conditions, change to the broader societal and political environment in which education is located and to which it is expected to contribute, may also alter the balance of purposes which education may be asked to pursue. The picture becomes further confused when we enquire as to who is, or should be, the prime beneficiary of the education process, student, employer or society (Golby 1987: 12–20; Watts 1985: 9–22) and in relation to this, who should bear the costs of education.

Not surprisingly, then, education is driven by, and is subject to, a complex of values, summarised by Kogan in terms of educational, social, economic and institutional values (Kogan 1985: 19). To these can be included a political perspective which, especially since the economic crises of the 1970s, has served to shape the educational value-system (Simon 1988: 11). Educational values can be traced to the tradition of fostering

> the individual's full range of ability and aptitudes, with the cultivation of spiritual and moral values, with the nurturing of imagination and sensibility, with the transmission and reinterpretation of culture.
>
> (Watts 1985: 9; see also Abbs 1987)

This approach has been largely embraced by an educational establishment which seeks broad, non-utilitarian development of the individual student as the central focus of its activities. In this sense, there may be no additional purpose to education; it can be regarded as a good in its own right, and answerable only to values intrinsic to education itself. This liberal approach links with those social values of education which promote equality of access and opportunity with a profound 'belief in the educability of all children' (Chitty 1986: 88) as expressed through comprehensive principles of education without pre-selection. As a consequence, perhaps, of this non-utilitarian stance, teachers have been

charged with possessing and transmitting an anti-commercial bias founded upon an ignorance towards and disdain for industrial work.

Institutional values relate more to the education process rather than
outcome (Kogan 1985: 21) but concern the degree and allocation of
influence, control and power over outcomes enjoyed by the principal
interest groups within and beyond the boundaries of education. Traditionally, most outcome influence within education has been at the
disposal of a hierarchy of education 'professionals' from the Department of Education, through local education authorities to teachers themselves. But recent ideological and political developments external to
education have led to a weakening of 'professional interest' influence
which has been conceded to centralised state control over the curriculum
and 'consumer' involvement in school governance (Ranson 1990:
10–17).

This shift derives mainly from the current emphasis given to an
economic orientation to education which assumes a more 'relevant' and
utilitarian educational purpose. In this latter sense, education is evaluated according to the contribution it makes to economic well-being
through building up the stock and quality of human inputs to economic
activity. Taking this view, educational expenditure is seen as a form of
'investment' from which a tangible rate of return can be sought.
Numerous studies which have set out to establish or measure
associations between productivity, level of earnings and educational
attainment have reported a positive return to education 'human capital'
(Blaug 1970). In the same tradition, studies have attempted to seek links
between education, levels and types of employment and national economic growth. At a different level of analysis, politicians and employers
have sought to associate alleged workplace 'indiscipline' (and hence,
poor productivity) and employability with purported inadequate attention paid by the teaching profession to fostering work-supportive 'attitudes' and discipline at school (Jamieson 1985: 28; Finn 1987: 121–3).

The British government has committed itself to undertake systematic
reform of the educational system by giving primacy to the economic
strand of the educational value-system. At the same time, both comprehensive principle and method has been under attack as the government
has sought to moderate the influence of social priorities which stress
equality and educational objectives promoting all-round individual
development. As these have been identified most closely with the
education 'professions', it is the teachers and local education authorities
which have borne the brunt of the government's reform programme
(Dale 1985: 45–6; Simon 1988; Flude and Hammer 1990).

The present movement for reform of education was stimulated by the speech given by the then Labour Prime Minister, James Callaghan, at Ruskin College, Oxford in 1976, which launched the so-called 'Great Debate' on the contemporary responsibilities of education. Earlier, reaction to comprehensive education had been mounted through a series of so-called Education Black Papers (1969–77) which pointed to the apparent lack of relevance to many children of education geared to the acquisition of academic qualifications. Academicism resulted in a lack of preparedness for work both in attitude and skill and hence a mismatch between employer requirements for young labour and the supply of that labour. The consequence it was contended, was alienated, unemployed youth. As economic difficulties mounted, and with them the emergence of mass unemployment in young people, the political clamour over the directions and responsibilities of education increased.

Education was pushed to the forefront of political activity, and pressures mounted for the education providers to: 'emphasise the contribution of the economy to national life and prepare pupils to take their place in that economy as it now exists. They should accept it and adapt to it as smoothly as possible' (Dale 1985: 3).

Education providers have been expected to conform to a market-orientated political climate by responding positively to the expressed needs – or 'market signals' – of 'consumers', these being students about to enter the labour market or industry itself. This instrumental approach requires teachers to be sympathetic to industry's needs and to transmit their enthusiasm to pupils. Hence, teachers are encouraged to spend periods in industry (perhaps during vacation time) in order to learn about 'the real world', and to arrange for pupils to become familiar with the attractions of local industry through visits or placements in plants, offices and factories. Industrial managers are encouraged to reciprocate by visiting schools and participating in classroom activities and through assuming responsibilities in school governance.

In consequence, the education services would be responsible for the preparation of young people for work in a changing society and in particular, for the provision of skills relevant to local demand with especial emphasis upon technology.

As a reinforcing inducement to educational reform, measures used to direct and assess commercial viability and workplace competence, such as strict financial control systems, observance of line management authority, appraisal systems and remuneration based on performance are also to be applied to education services increasingly exposed to the disciplines of the market economy in terms of student choice and funding. The national curriculum introduced by the 1988 Education Reform Act is an integral part of this approach. Published results from national assessments will illuminate the performance of schools, with high performers attracting pupils and thereby increasing funds allocated to schools under local management: 'Parents become consumers and schools are seen as suppliers of a product. If a school does not perform well . . . parents will take their custom elsewhere' (*Labour Research*, September 1990: 18).

The transition to a more vocationally based education system for the bulk of young people is expected to serve the immediate recipients in helping them to secure employment, to assist industry in resolving labour supply difficulties and benefit the nation in terms of production and economic growth.

THE VOCATIONAL PROGRAMME

Signs of the 'new vocationalism' are evident throughout education but are most visible at the level of secondary education, the traditional dividing line in Britain between continuation with an academically defined curriculum, represented by GCE 'O' and 'A' levels, and an early exit from education at the minimum age of 16 years for the less academically inclined.

Two major problems are presented by this early bifurcation of educational opportunity. First, for young people withdrawing from full-time education, there have been few alternative routes to continue education or to gain qualifications. Unless British youth is peculiarly untalented, there is little doubt that enormous losses in potential occur at this stage; full-time education participation rates beyond the minimum leaving age are currently estimated at 32 per cent, which with a further 16 per cent of 16–18-year-olds undertaking YTS, represents one of the lowest participation rates in Europe (Training Agency 1989: 14; Pearson *et al.* 1989: 6). Aside from the loss this drainage represents to individuals and society, this low figure also means that the base for continuation into post-compulsory and higher education is precariously narrow, which is reflected in low entrance rates (at most, 16 per cent of the population) to university level studies in the UK. This is occurring at a time when:

it has been estimated that by the end of the century, 70% of all jobs in the (European) Community will be carried out by so called brain workers, and of these activities, no less than 35% will require a university degree.

(Times Higher Education Supplement, 2 March 1990)

In the light of this disparity between the inputs required to serve the needs of a sophisticated economy and current attainments, the government's concern to increase participation in higher education is scarcely surprising and its commitment to double the number of students at this level over the next twenty-five years highly understandable (Pearson *et al.* 1990: 1). Demonstrating even greater ambition, the Labour Party, in its policy document, has announced its intentions of trebling the number of 18-year-olds with 'A' level equivalents by the year 2000 (Labour Policy Document 1990).

The second major problem concerns the 68 per cent of British young people not continuing with full-time studies after the age of 16 years, particularly as claims have been made that up to 40 per cent of these leave school with no formal educational qualifications (letter to the *Financial Times*, 17 March 1990). As demographic change forces employers to compete for the dwindling supply of young people it is possible that more of these will be tempted away from school at the earliest opportunity (or at least at age 18) and thereafter rely upon employer-based training as the basis for their future development (*Times Higher Education Supplement*, 2 March 1990). As we shall see, employer training provision has rarely offered a reliable or consistent platform for employees to obtain further qualifications, whilst personal growth has somewhat paradoxically been viewed by industry as the responsibility of education and received minimal attention from employers, unless linked directly to corporate needs (Fonda and Hayes 1986: 49).

The scale of the problem facing Britain can be judged from the experience of France, which, with a similar sized population, has been estimated to progress one-and-a-half times as many young people through education to age 18 than the UK. Further, the proportion of students achieving higher education entrance qualifications is higher in France (White 1988: 6–7). Similarly adverse comparisons of participation and attainment rates have been made with West Germany, a point which is developed further in Chapter 4 (Prais and Wagner 1985: 185–6).

As we have seen, critics of education provision contend that so many young people fail to benefit from education because the system is geared primarily to the delivery and acquisition of academic qualifications with little or no parallel provision for the low or late achiever, who may, none the less, possess or gain qualities also capable of receiving formal recognition. The words of a principal of a college of technology help to convey the depth of concern still felt by one closely involved with 'non-academic' students:

> We are still locked into an educational system which was and is built round the needs of an elite. Vocational education has always been seen as for the horny-handed and the low-browed: only academic qualification has mattered.
>
> (Letter to the *Guardian*, 15 March 1990)

The major challenges at school level which emerge from the deficiencies described above are first, how to broaden the coverage of education to ensure that a wider proportion of young people continue with their studies after the age of 16, and second, how to recognise and raise the range and levels of attainment within education to offer equivalent status for qualifications achieved by those not wanting or suited to traditional academic advancement in terms of 'O' and 'A' level qualifications.

The government has undertaken a number of initiatives which supporters contend do confront these major issues. One leading programme is the Technical and Vocational Education Initiative (TVEI), described as 'a major attempt by central government to shift the curriculum and pedagogy of the middle and upper years of secondary schooling (14–18-year-olds) away from the traditions of academic general education' (Fulton 1987: 102).

Introduced originally in pilot form in fourteen local education authorities (LEA) in England and Wales in 1983, the experiment was soon extended to the rest of the country, covering all LEAs by 1988. A ten-year programme to introduce the Initiative to all maintained schools and colleges was announced by the government in 1986.

The TVEI differs from previous educational initiatives on a number of scores: first, it was introduced and subsequently co-ordinated through the Manpower Services Commission (MSC), which was itself part of the Department of Employment, rather than through the Department of Education and Science. This decision had 'strong symbolic significance, with the Commission being seen as a new broom with direct links to employers and trade unions, and not hidebound by undue respect for tradition' (Fulton 1987: 104). Second, the scheme was promoted to dispel the second class stigma of vocational education by offering equal status between academic and vocational preparation through its designation for the whole ability range. Third, the vocational element would be enhanced by programmes designed to apply personal, interpersonal and transferable skills to the resolution of work-based problems. Direct contact with local employers and their needs would be encouraged through work visits, 'shadowing' and placements. Particular emphasis would be given to the development of 'enterprise' and 'initiative'.

Since the introduction of the programme in 1983, there has been little opportunity for comprehensive evaluation of its impact, mainly because of the continually developing nature of the project and the wide diversity of programmes introduced by different institutions. The local authorities, and indeed individual institutions, have been offered sufficient discretion, within limits, to develop their own programmes, guided by local need, experience and culture. Hence, Fulton reports that in some schools, only about a quarter of curriculum time might be allocated to TVEI; in others, up to 70 per cent of time can be offered to the scheme. This in turn can affect recruitment to the programme, with the more strongly academic students tending to reject concentrated TVEI programmes in favour of traditional studies (Fulton 1987: 106). The original MSC objective of appealing to a wide range of ability could well be compromised by the proportion of school time allocated to TVEI, compounded, of course, by the nature and emphases of the curriculum on offer (Tenne 1987).

Even in terms of its stated objectives, experience with TVEI appears to be mixed and studies so far do not demonstrate marked short-term improvement in employer satisfaction with school-leavers; however, it may take rather longer for the anticipated transferable skills and self-motivation effects of TVEI to make an impact at work, and even then, any positive effects attributable to TVEI may become, in time, masked by other changes, such as improved training provision by employers.

Initial student reactions to TVEI have been examined; in particular evaluations of the scheme in preparing them for adult life have been undertaken. In one survey of 3,000 16–17-year-olds a sample of ex-TVEI students compared their fifth form study experiences against those of non-participants and a higher proportion of the former reported that their studies had provided useful preparation for working life (Helsby 1989). But without detail of response rate or levels of uniformity between the groups, their educational record and treatment, it would be premature to conclude that TVEI was responsible for creating work compatibility, especially in the absence of confirmation from employers.

Matched ability groups of 1,000 TVEI and 1,000 non-scheme participants showed a considerably higher proportion of the latter continued with full-time post-compulsory education (49.6 per cent to 38.3 per cent) and from those that left school at 16, a higher proportion (32.8 per cent) of ex-TVEI participants undertook the government's Youth Training Scheme (YTS), more than double the national average of 16 per cent for the age group (Helsby 1989: 89, Training Agency 1989: 14). Full details of the experiences of the two groups are shown in Fig. 2.1. If the aim of the Initiative is to increase post-16 education participation rates, then these early figures are not too encouraging.

Figure 2.1 Post-16 destinations of TVEI students

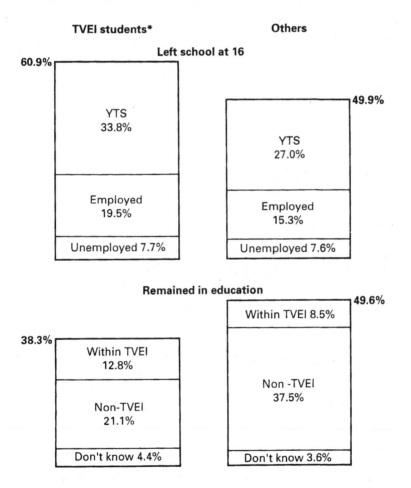

Note: * Unclassified: TVEI – 0.8 per cent, others 0.5 per cent.
Source: Helsby 1989: 79

The same study indicates that TVEI participants may be less academically inclined than non-participants, calling into question the scheme's objective of drawing upon students from the full ability range. Nevertheless, Helsby reports that there are signs that TVEI students are beginning to accumulate vocational qualifications after the age of 16, a process which should be assisted by the establishment of the National Council for Vocational Qualifications (NCVQ) in 1986 and its heroic efforts to rationalise the massively diverse range of non-academic qualifications into a coherent, standardised hierarchy, recognised throughout England and Wales, and compatible with equivalent Scottish qualifications. Table 2.1 shows the grading structure and their equivalence in academic qualifications. It is through this hierarchy that the government plans to substantially increase the proportion of qualified young people.

TVEI is also expected to avoid gender stereotyping, but a preliminary study indicates that this was not always achieved with early student

Table 2.1: National Vocational Qualifications (NVQs)

NVQ Level I

Shows competence in the performance of a range of work activities which are primarily routine and predictable, or provide a broad foundation, primarily as a basis for progression.

NVQ Level II

Shows competence in a broader and more demanding range of work activities involving greater individual responsibility and autonomy than at Level I. For setting national targets academic qualifications equivalent to 5 GCSEs at grades A–C or better match this level.

NVQ Level III

Shows competence in skilled areas that involve performance of a broad range of work activities, including many that are complex and non- routine. In some areas, supervisory competence may be a requirement at this level. Academic qualifications equivalent to a portfolio of 2 'A' levels plus 5 GCSEs at grades A–C or better are the comparable level for target purposes.

NVQ Level IV

Shows competence in the performance of complex, technical, specialised and professional work activities including those associated with design, planning and problem-solving, normally carrying a significant degree of personal accountability. In many areas competence in supervision or management will be a requirement at this level.

intakes to the programme. Girls were over-represented in subjects such as home economics and boys tended towards craft, design and technology and the applied aspects of science and computer studies (Tenne 1987: 522). A worrying feature is that the extension of the programme is not being matched by equivalent expenditures on TVEI: from a level of up to £80,000 annually per school for the early initiatives, projected maximum expenditure is now not expected to exceed £30,000 per annum (Fulton 1987: 102). These reductions will invariably curtail institutional scope for teaching innovation, one of the commonly agreed successful areas of the scheme so far and, crucially, restrict access to resources for updating the technology upon which the relevance and attraction of many projects is dependent.

These early findings raise suspicions in the minds of educational critics about the underlying motivations of the government in pushing developments in vocational education and the TVEI in particular. These argue that rather than offering equivalence to vocational qualifications in a coherent education strategy, vocational schemes form an integral part of the ideological thrust against public provision of services. Successive reductions in educational expenditure in alliance with recent sustained offensives against (public sector) teaching unions would seem to be consistent with this approach (Simon 1980). These critics further contend that narrowly based vocational programmes whose purpose is to segregate young people at an early age have the effect of reducing life opportunities (still heavily dependent on academic qualifications) rather than expanding them. For this reason many educationalists have expressed severe reservations about government plans to introduce twenty city technological colleges (CTC), which have the expressed intention of serving local industry needs by encouraging commercial sponsorship for segregated schools outwith LEA control. As ever, however, industry's response to this invitation has been muted, though whether this is through not wishing to directly interfere in educational matters or through unwillingness to pay for the service is not known. To date, only three CTCs have opened, heavily endorsed with government rather than industry funding (*Labour Research*, April 1990: 8–10).

For many in education, the supremacy of economic motives as the educational driving force is itself restrictive, and ultimately self-defeating as young people will be presented with limited programmes tailored to current, localised, employer needs as opposed to future societal needs. Just as industry shows little interest in broadening the horizons of employees, education in the service of industry will have similarly limited aspirations; indeed a wider educative purpose might be considered with some hostility: 'if we have a highly educated and idle population, we may possibly anticipate more serious social conflict. People must be educated once more to know their place' (DES official quoted in Chitty 1986: 94).

In turn, however, these short-term considerations impact negatively upon the wider economy as industry desperately competes for sufficient numbers of people educated to the levels demanded by a highly technological dynamic society. In particular, this future demand will be concentrated toward people educated to degree standard or its equivalent.

HIGHER EDUCATION

Higher education faces major challenges with regard to both quantity and nature of its 'output'. We pointed out earlier that both major political parties in Britain are committed to radical expansion of student numbers over the next few years. By international standards, the 15 or 16 per cent of Britain's 17–19-year-olds who enter higher education is small, though a high proportion of these (about 80 per cent after three years of study) do graduate. Other countries tend to adopt a different emphasis, providing wider entrance opportunity, but risking higher withdrawal and failure rates. This is particularly the case with the USA where entrance rates are about 58 per cent of the eligible age group, but only about half actually stay on to graduate, sometimes requiring many years to do so (DES 1989: 30). Nevertheless, the UK system stands accused of being elitist and segregationist in its pursuit of academic quality for a minority of participants. For social equity reasons alone, there are strong arguments for widening student access.

Of growing concern to the government and industry, however, are the economic pressures for more graduates. Figure 2.2 shows projected changes in occupational employment up to 1995. It shows that the most profound change will be in the demands for professional, technical and managerial occupations, precisely those occupations that many companies are currently short of (Ball 1990: 8; Hyman and Bell 1989). Competition for graduates is likely to sharpen as professional mobility increases within the European Economic Community. Already, many engineering and technology courses are providing language study as an integral part of the curriculum, and European educational placements have become more commonplace as the Erasmus programme for Community education projects grows in popularity (see *Times Higher Education Supplement*, 25 May 1990).

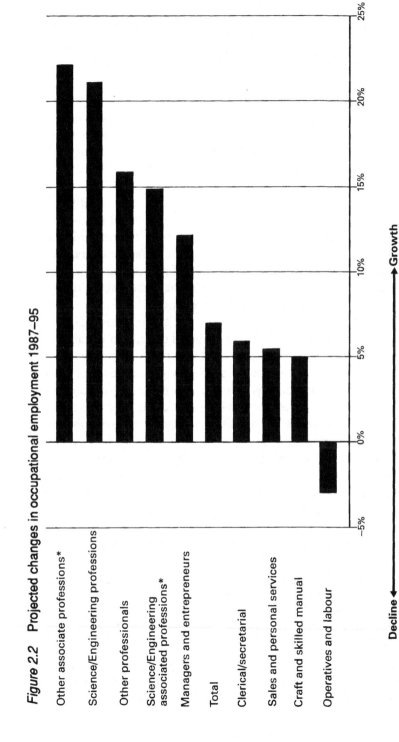

Figure 2.2 Projected changes in occupational employment 1987–95

Note: * e.g. technicians, paramedics, computer programmers, legal executives.
Source: Ball 1990: 9

In addition to a projected general deficiency of educated manpower required for a sophisticated and dynamic economy, a number of specific occupational shortages have become apparent; teachers and engineers, in particular, are in short supply (Cassels 1990: 10). There are real dangers that economic growth and adaptability will be compromised unless action is taken to increase the output of qualified people in Britain. To make matters worse, a number of competitor countries, already with higher participation rates than the UK, are taking steps to expand further the proportion of young people who satisfy university entrance requirements (Cassels 1990: 46).

While growing shortages of specific occupational qualifications become more evident, Britain suffers from an additional short-coming: the numbers of well-qualified people who are entering and participating in management. Two problems become apparent; the first concerns the educational background of managers. The first column in Table 2.2 shows comparisons between the educational attainments of senior managers from the UK and competitor countries.

Many commentators have suggested that the poor overall qualifications of Britain's managers has contributed directly to Britain's poor economic performance. There are also indirect effects: poorly educated managers might not recognise or acknowledge the value of qualifications gained by subordinates or applicants, preferring instead to rely upon a combination of instinct and experience in choosing and promoting staff. Also, the likelihood of such managers endorsing the values of continuing development in their organisations may be diminished. Indeed, there may be insufficient recognition of the innovative and flexibility benefits associated with systematic training and development, and these could even be viewed as potential threats to managers' own security and authority. Moreover, it would be surprising if graduates were to be intimidated by learning new techniques and processes: languages and new technology are not likely to pose major problems to people accustomed to systematic learning schedules and may well be welcomed by them.

The second perceived problem relates to management qualifications. The final column of Table 2.2 shows that comparatively few British managers have studied for specific business qualifications, such as MBA. This situation has rung alarm bells in both education and among professional management organisations, and both have set out to expand the range of business and management qualifications in Britain: these developments are examined in greater depth in Chapter 5.

Table 2.2: Educational attainments of senior managers

Countries	Top managers with degree (%)	Numbers of qualified accountants (000s)	MBAs per annum
Britain	24[1]	120.0*	1,200**
USA	85[2]	300.0 (est.)	70,000
West Germany	62[3]	3.8	0
France	65[4]	20.0 (est.)	0[†]
Japan	85[5]	6.0	60

Data from:
[1] M. Koudra, Management training, practice and attitudes, BIM Management Survey report 1975; [2] Survey by Korn Ferry Int, 1986; [3] H. Evers and G. Landsberg, Qualifikation und Kariere Deutsches Institut, 1982; [4] INSEE National Statistics Office; [5] Survey by Tokyo Keizai Magazine.

* Accountants working in Britain – combined estimates of six professional bodies.
** British nationals.
[†] INSEAD graduates not included. It is not part of the French system.

Source: Handy *et al.* 1988: 3.

There is no question, therefore, that higher education is in need of expansion and government is aware of the seriousness of the need. Unfortunately, State provision cannot be achieved without cost and strong competition for resources in other areas of education and for other services such as the medical and pension requirements of an ageing population (Williams 1990: 258) has led the government to explore alternative means to stimulate and resource an expanded student population. If the government is serious in its intention to expand the numbers entering higher education, a higher proportion of young people must gain appropriate entrance qualifications. These, of course, have been dominated by the traditional academic 'A' levels, but wider access could be achieved by widening the acceptability of alternative qualifications, such as those offered by the Business and Technician Education Council (BTEC) or the NCVQ (see *Financial Times*, 2 January 1991). A second move to broaden the range of potential students would be to embrace more mature students with further opening of entrance qualifications to include work and social experience. Qualifications could be increased through part-time study and through distance learning techniques. These would not be eligible for government support and would be paid for by some combination of student and employer financing.

For full-time students a new (for Britain) approach to the funding of advanced studies has been adopted. The government has determined that higher educational expansion must be financed through contributions from the immediate recipients in the form of loans, which supplement the existing frozen maintenance grant. With inflation, the loans element is expected to grow to a maximum half of the student's financial support by the year 2007/8.

A loans system is also expected to integrate with wider labour market signals through encouraging students to pursue courses linked to high paying (and presumably short supply) occupations. The government has also made moves to adjust supply-side factors in order to facilitate an effective response from 'providers' through granting independent corporate status to public sector institutions (polytechnics and institutes of higher education) released from local authority control. Executive boards of these institutions now exercise considerable financial and strategic autonomy.

The government has made known that the greater emphasis given to 'enterprise', 'initiative' and entrepreneurship should find expression in advanced as well as lower level studies. A Higher Enterprise Initiative was launched in 1987 to provide funding for institutions to develop innovative teaching methods geared to industry needs. In particular, work-based projects, placements and experience are encouraged through the Initiative.

Government encouragement of closer ties between education and industry is expressed in other diverse ways. Under the 1988 Education Reform Act, governing bodies of maintained further education colleges are required to draw at least half of their membership from 'employment interests'. The duties and responsibilities of these governing bodies point to more strategic inputs by them into financing, staffing and course provision and rather less involvement by Local Education Authorities in college affairs (Unwin 1990: 246). These moves are paralleled by developments in the newly independent higher education institutes; almost half of the governors appointed as independent members of executive bodies have been company directors (270 from 564). A further 22 per cent have been company managers or professionals such as accountants and management consultants. Only ten trade unionists have received appointments (*NATFHE Journal* 1989: 17).

Department of Trade and Industry calls for closer collaboration between industry and higher education have been made through a series of glossy publications aimed at corporate managers. For education, the call has been to go to industry for research funding. As a consequence, industry funding of research has increased from £47.4 million in 1984–5 to £76.9 million in 1987–8, an increase of 62 per cent over the four years (AUT 1989: 11). As a proportion of gross domestic product, however, overall expenditure on research and development remained virtually static over this period, owing to a growth in government expenditure of only 28 per cent (AUT 1989: 20).

The overall impact is that Britain's place in R & D expenditure remains firmly anchored near the bottom of the league.

CONCLUDING COMMENTS

Government industrial relations policy is geared to stimulating market forces through extending the proportion of economic activity served by the private sector, by making supply factors more sensitive to market pressures and by encouraging private sector involvement in responding to market demands for factors of production.

Manifestation of this policy can be witnessed at various levels of educational provision. Of particular relevance is the encouragement by the government to employers to involve themselves in educational matters, and to realign educational output to meet economic demands. This approach is reinforced through distancing trade unions from circles of educational influence. In addition to the market, however, the government maintains close control over the context in which education operates.

This context is becoming increasingly vocational or instrumental, in that education is expected to express and represent employer needs. The government is prepared to give employers the lead in promoting education in the hope that future industry needs will be met through closer association with education. Whether education should be directed in such ways is a major issue currently being debated in educational and academic circles, for it is by no means certain that economic success is dependent upon a heavy vocational bias within education; whether employers are capable or prepared to act as the educational catalyst envisaged by the government is the major practical question. British employers have a poor record in promoting vocational education and training; among managers, only a minority have received higher education, and training for them has been a comparative rarity.[1] Nevertheless, as part of its overall policy programme, the government has extended this trust to substantially increase employer involvement in contemporary manpower policy, and it is to this area which we turn in the following chapter.

Chapter 3

Manpower policy

We'll train the workers without jobs to do the jobs without workers.
(Government publicity for Employment Training)

Education serves a unique public purpose in preparing people for full and active participation in public life; not only as producers and consumers but as citizens with rights and obligations, the exercise of which is heavily contingent upon the educational process for their comprehension and activation. For this reason, education can be considered a democratic prerogative, requiring a minimum level of access available openly to all members of the national community. Interested parties may differ over their interpretations of 'minimum access' but few would argue against the proposition itself or against the view that democratic principles become meaningless symbols in the absence of a freely available education service.

To meet these universal objectives of education requires government to be responsible for its financing and overall supervision, whereas the directions taken by manpower policy – over decisions concerned with co-ordinating labour inputs with the aggregated processes of production of goods and services – can display greater variety, formed from the political and economic context from which production decisions arise. The potential dimensions of manpower policy can be seen as a continuum extending from full intervention by the State through a centralised system of planned production to virtual State abstention dominated by reliance upon market autonomy to allocate both inputs and outcomes from the production process. A political shift toward free-market thinking is likely to be associated with parallel moves toward State abstention from supply-side intervention. The British governmental approach has typically been oriented toward the market end of this continuum, encouraging labour supply arrangements to be regulated through a multitude of voluntary decisions by employers and employees, who individually would be expected to respond rationally to market signals to provide and acquire skills in short supply. For this reason, this approach has been designated as 'voluntarist' and the State, as policy-maker, largely abstains from direct interference in labour and skills allocations.

Nevertheless, occasions arise when change taking place in the broader economy demands a more co-ordinated and direct response than that offered through the complex interplay of product and labour market operations. Two particular occasions when the British government adopted a more interventionist approach stand out. First, national crises of production during the First and Second World Wars were largely averted through the recruitment of unskilled men and women into jobs for which training was provided through State training programmes. Once the immediate emergency of war-time lifted, however, the State reverted to its more traditional passive stance (Sheldrake and Vickerstaffe 1987).

A more recent intervention was initiated in the mid-1960s: economic growth was failing to keep pace with that of competitor markets, making the domestic economy vulnerable to balance of trade and inflationary crises. To increase British competitiveness a policy of economic restructuring was embarked upon, founded largely upon encouraging rationalisation through corporate mergers and take-overs in order to gain economy of scale advantages. Co-operation for change was sought by the government through drawing both the TUC and the newly created CBI into the overall management of the economy as national policy was shifted from a voluntary to a consensus-based planning model.

To minimise opposition at factory level by those most at risk from these major changes and to gain a measure of employee commitment to them, legislation was passed which provided redundancy payments for displaced workers and this was reinforced by a State-led training programme to absorb lost jobs and to prepare the nation's workforce for the new tasks demanded by the imminent 'white hot technological revolution'.

The Industry Training Act (1964) and its associated Industry Training Boards (ITBs) were established both to provide greater numbers of higher skilled workers in British industry and to ensure equitable distribution of the costs of training by requiring concerns 'in scope' to a particular industry to pay a levy, usually based on a head-count of employees, repayable as a grant if approved training was provided by the employer. This approach was adopted in an attempt to reduce the levels of poaching used by some employers to further their supply of skills, and which represented an additional blow to the non-interventionist free-market approach to manpower policy: a 'rational' employer might satisfy immediate skill needs by buying in requirements as and when needed rather than through lengthy and potentially risky expenditure on training.

At their peak in the early 1970s there were twenty-seven Boards covering over half the nation's workforce. However, by posing a direct challenge to the voluntarist doctrine Training Boards failed to gain the support of employers who remained apprehensive of State interference in the conduct of their employment relations. The statutory powers of the Boards were first curtailed by legislation in 1973 and in 1982, as part of the return to voluntarism, the majority of the ITBs were abolished under the Industrial Training Act, leaving just seven major Boards covering about one quarter of the workforce. The most recent government proposals aim to convert these surviving Boards into independent voluntary training bodies; the experiment in intervention had been relatively short lived, though, in terms of training provision, not altogether unsuccessful (IDS 1980; Sheldrake and Vickerstaffe 1987: 36).

The Conservative government elected in 1979 faced a major dilemma; ideologically committed to a market-led economy, with minimal interference with its operation, it has been confronted by developments which challenge the capability of a voluntarist system to cope adequately with major changes taking place within the economy. The past ten years witnessed first, a politically unacceptable surge in unemployment among young people, and more latterly, growing signs that Britain is falling further behind her trading partners in training and vocational educational provision. Increasingly, it has become apparent that economic progress is suffering through skill shortages and in the absence of sustained corrective action, the outlook for the future appears equally pessimistic.

The initial governmental response was to construct a programme consistent with the belief that market failure was attributable to inadequate attention to supply-side support. The means used to liberalise the labour market and to suppress the purported inhibiting effects of trade unions on the free operation of this market has been discussed earlier, as has the attempt to manoeuvre education into more commercially oriented supply-side directions (see Chapter 2).

Nevertheless, manpower policy, the last remaining bastion of voluntarism, was still confronted with the difficulty of remaining faithful to non-interventionist principles yet dealing with the embarrassingly high numbers of people for whom such an approach appeared to render little assistance. The solution was to compromise by introducing government-backed programmes for the most vulnerable members of the labour force, the unemployed and young people wishing to enter work, but to keep faith with market forces for those already in employment. Even the first of these approaches, however, did not depart far from the voluntarist doctrine as it placed considerable reliance upon the (voluntary) willingness of employers both to take part in publicly-sponsored schemes and when participating, to give them the responsibility to provide training of a quality and quantity to match the stated requirements of the programmes. Nevertheless, early schemes emerging from the recession of the late 1970s had limited ambitions: whilst providing a veneer of training provision, approaches such as the much-criticised Youth Opportunities Programme (1978–83) had largely been used to provide short-term work experience programmes at temptingly low cost to employers (Short 1986: 42–6; Chapman and Tooze 1987: 45–7).

By the early 1980s, the formal emphasis was altered to offer programmes which aimed to enhance employability through offering skills training, primarily to young people and more recently to longer-term unemployed adults. Two schemes have dominated government funding and practice since this period; first, the Youth Training Scheme (YTS) and more latterly, Employment Training (ET) for adults. For 1989/90 it was estimated that nearly 90 per cent of the government's £2.6 billion budget was scheduled to be allocated to the two programmes (Training Agency 1989: 91). As these schemes have represented the main thrust of manpower policy and both are highly dependent upon employer support for their acceptance, it is worthwhile to consider their development and operation in some detail.

Both programmes can trace their genesis to the New Training Initiative (NTI) launched by the MSC in 1981. Three broad objectives formed the basis to this programme:

1 The development of skill training, including apprenticeship, in such a way as to enable people entering at different ages and with different educational attainments to acquire agreed standards of skill appropriate to the jobs available and to provide them with a basis for progression through further learning.
2 Movement towards a position where all young people under the age of 18 have the opportunity either of continuing in full-time education or of entering a period of planned work experience combined with work-related training and education.

3 Widespread opportunities for adults whether employed or returning to work, to acquire, increase or update their skills and knowledge during the course of their working lives.

(MSC 1981)

In practice, greater priority was given initially to the first two of these objectives as the government struggled to deal with the economic and social consequences of mass unemployment among young people. The one-year Youth Training Scheme (YTS) was introduced in 1983 and subsequently extended to two years for 16–17-year-olds in 1986. The YTS was largely employer-based, offering a combination of planned work experience with on-the-job training supplemented by a minimum of 20 weeks off-the-job training over the two years. Intake to the programme fluctuated between 350,000 and 400,000 trainees annually and about a quarter of all 16-year-olds started on the programme.

YTS was introduced with three main objectives, aiming, respectively, at the level of individual trainees, participating employer and toward the national interest:

1 To provide all young participants with . . . an integrated programme of training, education and work experience . . . which can serve as a foundation for subsequent employment or continued training or relevant further education.
2 To provide a better equipped young workforce for the participating employer.
3 To develop and maintain a versatile, readily adaptable, highly motivated and productive workforce for Britain.

(Chapman and Tooze 1987: 52)

Publicity pronouncements have tended to emphasise the suitability of YTS for *quality* training appropriate to the needs of an advanced technological and competitive business environment (Training Agency 1988). Success in meeting this aim, however, hinges upon attracting employer support, first of all, to participate in the scheme, and second, to provide 'quality' training associated with the scheme. The extent to which these objectives have been met by employers is discussed further in Chapter 7.

There is, of course, a further requirement for scheme success, and that pertains to its suitability to meet stated objectives. One problem is that the hierarchy of aims identified above for YTS are not necessarily compatible; to provide individual trainees with high-quality transferable skills demanded by a sophisticated economy would require high government expenditure to compensate employers who individually might have little to gain from providing trainees with marketable skills. Many of the criticisms aimed at YTS point to inadequacy of funding as a prime source of its modest achievements (Marsden and Ryan 1989: 52). Limitations in government support could deter employer participation in the programme unless tangible benefits to them could be anticipated. Young people would be loathe to enter if allowances were set too low or if the schemes failed to live up to expectations in providing useful skills and negotiable qualifications. The approach adopted to deal with this problem was to severely restrict the voluntary element for trainees, who subsequently risked losing benefit if they 'unreasonably' turned down an offer of a place on YTS and by relaxation of the supervision imposed on employers to maintain high training standards, notwithstanding the formal commitment given to quality and transferability (Lee et al. 1990: 186–95). At the same time much of the promotion for YTS took the form of publicising its benefits to employers in terms of employment screening and low costs of labour.

The limited impact in meeting quality objectives can be measured by the overall lack of qualifications gained by participants. Over three-quarters of trainees leaving the scheme between April 1986 and January 1988 failed to gain a single qualification and though the position has improved following the development of the two-year scheme, most of the qualifications gained by the 40 per cent of trainees who secured them are at the lower levels of the NVCQ scale (Jones 1988: 65).

The failure of YTS to have a marked effect on approved qualifications has in turn led to two sets of criticisms: first, the extent of skill transferability obtained by trainees during their training period could be limited as employers concentrate on using trainees to help satisfy specific production requirements (Lee et al. 1990); second, and as a consequence, the programme's relevance to an economy attempting to come to terms with an increasingly technologically skill-based work environment needs to be questioned. Other critics who have examined the scheme's commitment to trainee-centredness point to a lack of equal opportunity; rather than opening doors for young women to enter occupations and industries in which they are under-represented, YTS placements have tended to follow well-established employment patterns which reinforce existing gender inequalities (Cockburn 1987; Lee et al. 1990: 61–2). Similarly, opportunities for young people from ethnic minorities appear to be restricted (Asher 1989). The limitations to the voluntary status of YTS, coupled with continual financial restrictions, would have done little to expand either commitment to the scheme by young people coerced into it, opportunities for their development or the overall levels of qualifications.

It appears that the government has acknowledged the substance of these criticisms by taking steps to revamp YTS within a new localised delivery framework described in more detail below. YTS has now been replaced by Youth Training (YT) which focuses more sharply on the attainment of nationally recognised vocational qualifications. All YT participants will have the opportunity to achieve vocational qualifications through the NCVQ framework. The main changes are that employed young people will be able to apply for participation on YT, it is no longer restricted to a maximum two-year format and the emphasis has shifted toward qualifications and to continuing development. An additional innovation is a trainee-centred voucher system involving the provision of training credits to the value of £1,500 for 16- and 17-year-olds, which has been advocated by the CBI and is currently undergoing pilot trials in selected areas.

For workless adults, the main approach adopted has been through Employment Training (ET), which was launched in September 1988 amidst a fanfare of publicity and the avowed declaration that: 'We'll train the workers without jobs to do the jobs without workers'. The implication was that problems of skill shortages could be remedied through the new training programmes. Existing adult support schemes were wound up and their finances pooled in order to resource the new £1.5 billion project. This meant that no additional money was being allocated to ET. The initial aim of the programme was to provide an average six months' training for long-term (6–12 months) adult unemployed, concentrating on the 18–24 age group. Training plans are drawn up by an independent training agent in consultation with individual clients, who are subsequently referred to a training manager charged with responsibility for organising the training schedule, with an employer or through project work. At least 40 per cent of the placement time is scheduled for 'directed training'. During the training period, participants receive a small (£10–£12) allowance in addition to their normal benefit payments. Though it is not compulsory for unemployed people to join the programme, moral persuasion is applied through invitations to attend regular interviews with Department of Employment officials through the Restart programme, which could lead to referral to ET. Unreasonable failure to attend a Restart interview could give grounds for withdrawal of benefit. This sanction coupled with continuing interest by government ministers in the American 'Workfare' system, in which benefit is contingent upon participation in approved work experience or training programmes, led to concern among trade unions and Labour politicians as to the ultimate intentions held for the ET programme.

Not surprisingly, from its very beginnings, ET was dogged by controversy. No new funding was provided, despite growing numbers of long-term unemployed. An annual throughput of 600,000 trainees was planned, representing an increase of 200,000 people annually above the aggregated numbers of people on earlier schemes. Under these circumstances, a persistent worry to be articulated concerned the quality of the training to be provided. Unions further believed that the scheme was geared primarily to removing unemployed people from the register at modest cost to the government and argued that adults performing work during training should receive a wage equal to the rate for the job and not an allowance to supplement benefit payments.

The government might have anticipated opposition from trade unions and their sympathisers; they were possibly not so prepared for the criticisms and doubts expressed by employers with regard to the scheme. It was 'unrealistic and inappropriate' for employers to provide training for jobless adults opined one contributor to *Personnel Management*, the Institute of Personnel Management professional journal, on the grounds that employers are expected to serve a commercial function and not the social one of providing placements for unemployed adults (1988: 6).

Other employer complaints were that the scheme, centred upon a tailored training plan for participants, was geared ostensibly towards the identified and specific needs of individual trainees and these needs might not conform to the patterns of local labour market demand. Some employers also objected to paying a contribution, totalling about £5 a day, for trainees.

Representatives of individual industries also expressed reservations. Manufacturing companies were still shedding labour when the scheme commenced, were not looking for new labour and if they were training, this was focused more to retraining their remaining employees for reconstituted internal needs. Only the construction and retail industries, who were experiencing labour shortages, expressed much enthusiasm for the new arrangements (*Financial Times*, 2 September 1988).

Nevertheless, it was the combined opposition of the major unions with interests in the public sector which comprised the major threat to the successful introduction and operation of the programme, as public sector support would be vital to ensure an adequate supply of work-based places for the scheme to function. In a motion to the 1988 annual conference of the TUC, public sector unions urged Congress not to support the scheme, a motion which though carried, offered sufficient ambiguity to provide the government time and space to remove the main obstacles to union endorsement and participation. The government's response was to wind up first the governing body of the Training Commission (the renamed MSC) and subsequently the Commission itself, a development which removed: 'the last forum through which the TUC and the Confederation of British Industry jointly exerted some control over important aspects of government policy' (*Financial Times*, 16 September 1988). From now, and with the creation of the Training Agency as an arm of the Department of Employment, the government would go it alone with its market-based policy.

ET continued to suffer difficulties: by early 1989, the number of places on offer was cut by 10 per cent due to the low take-up rate. The quality of training provided was continually exposed to questioning through press and media comment, culminating in the House of Commons all-party Employment Committee Report which condemned the spectacular drop-out rate from ET, in which nearly half (45 per cent) of those referred to the programme never arrived to take up their places and of those that did commence training, almost three-quarters withdrew before the conclusion of the programme. There was little evidence that trainees were encouraged to gain externally validated qualifications, despite this being one of the declared intentions of the scheme. Of the minority that did complete ET, nearly half returned to unemployment. The Committee confirmed that the main problem with the programme was one of under-funding (Employment Committee 1990). The introduction of private sector dominated Training and Enterprise Councils (see below) has given the opportunity for an overhaul of the ET scheme which, whilst retaining its original contours, is now expected to become more flexible and responsive to local employer needs in terms of length of training period and in meeting local skill deficiencies. Unfortunately, these developments have coincided with a period of rising inflation and high interest rates, both of which are placing severe pressures on the government to further reduce public project expenditure; to the dismay of the embryo Training and Enterprise Councils, one consequence has been a reduction in the amount of money available for government manpower interventions.

Notwithstanding the weaknesses associated with an absence of central involvement in helping to regulate the effects of a turbulent economic environment, since 1988 we have seen an intensification of market-led training in the UK. As mentioned above, the Manpower

Services Commission, operating as a tripartite body since 1973 to co-ordinate national manpower policy-making, was abruptly wound up following union opposition to the ET programme, re-emerging subsequently as the Training Agency, but under direct control of the Department of Employment. The main objectives of this body are as follows:

1   To encourage employers to train their staffs.
2   To provide and encourage training and vocational qualifications for young people in the transition from full-time education to work.
3   To help the unemployed (especially long-term) to gain skills, experience and enterprise which will help them find employment.
4   To help the education system to become more relevant to working life and more responsive to changing needs and opportunities in the labour market.
5   To encourage enterprise by offering support to small and independent concerns.
6   To decentralise training provision to 'local planning delivery and co-ordination of training'.

(Training Agency 1989: 90–2)

The broad educational directions taken by the Training Agency programme have been considered earlier. The pivotal feature of its manpower intentions concerns the first and sixth of these objectives, namely its proposed approach toward training for people in employment and its plans to decentralise government-sponsored training. With regard to employed members of the labour force, the approach remains very little changed: voluntarism supported by exhortation to both employers and employees to intensify their training efforts, but with little governmental funding, has been and continues to be the prime approach adopted, representing the purist market-led end of government policy.

The Training Agency's final objective also relies to a greater extent than previously upon market signals as a prime factor in determining training provision, with planning and delivery of training and enterprise programmes to be devolved to a network of about 100 local Training and Enterprise Councils (TECs) in England and Wales and to equivalent Local Enterprise Companies (LECs) for Scotland. Each of these bodies will assume wider responsibility for local training functions than those previously undertaken by the abolished Area Manpower Boards of the MSC, for which they receive an equivalent budget and Training Agency staff on secondment. Each TEC will be expected to take over and develop existing ET and YT programmes for its designated locality in a contractual relationship with the Training Agency. The boards of the TECs and LECs will be dominated by employer interests, with two-thirds of places allocated to senior management representatives drawn from the local business community. The intention is to delegate authority for training provision to TECs/LECs and for these to assume the training and developmental supervision previously undertaken by the more pluralist MSC/TC. To a considerable extent, government-backed training is being handed over to employers to organise.

CONCLUDING COMMENTS

As with education, current manpower policy places greater than ever faith upon employers to adopt an approach to training and development which enhances their own involvement, both through active participation in publicly-sponsored schemes such as YT and ET and by providing opportunities for the voluntary training and development of their own staffs. In other words, the practices and intentions of employers are crucial factors in determining the immediate destiny of the government's manpower policy and in turn, the skills, expertise and qualifications of the nation's workforce. Two questions which can be raised at this point concern the role of employers: first we need to ask to what extent such faith in employers can be justified.

We can start to explore this question by considering in more depth current employer training and development practices. These arrangements form part of, and indeed, emerge from the broader contexts of employment relations and systems of management operating within companies, which in turn mirror the wider commercial environments in which organisations function. Training and development as practised by employers can only be properly considered within a framework which offers full recognition to these factors.

The second question relates to the first though touches upon rather more complex issues; we need to ask whether the market-orientated approach which has dominated UK manpower policy is capable of remedying the deficiencies in skills, qualifications and abilities demanded by a technological society. To develop the medical metaphor often used to describe the state of the nation's economic health, we have identified symptoms of disease, but how appropriate is the treatment offered for curing the disease, rather than acting as a palliative which serves to relieve but not remove the presenting symptoms? Short-term treatment of current skill deficiencies runs the risk of plugging gaps but fails to offer a comprehensive, lasting, yet flexible approach to encourage the country to produce effectively with benefit to both producers and consumers. Extended discussion on this point is deferred to the final chapter. First, we return to our first question; to what extent can training provision be entrusted primarily to employers? To try and answer this, we need to examine the record of employers in providing training both in this country and overseas.

Chapter 4

Training policies and practices in other countries

High-quality basic education and vocational training are essential if the citizens of the Member States of the (European) Community are to meet the new challenges and take advantage of the new opportunities. They are real investments. The future of the Community depends on the skills and performance of its working population.

(CEDEFOP 1990)

Asked about the educational levels of the workforce at Toyota Motor, a senior director at the company surprised his American visitor by replying that about 80% literacy had been achieved. In explanation, the director continued: 'I don't mean an ability to read. I mean the ability to programme a computer-controlled machine. About 80% of our workers can do that. We hope to reach 100%.'

(Reported in the *Financial Times*, 3 December 1990)

INTRODUCTION

A representative analysis of training policies, arrangements and experience in other countries would fill a book on its own. Even then, problems would remain: Which countries to choose for illustration? How much detail to include on national political, industrial relations, education and manpower practices, all of which, to different degrees, feed into the training system? How to develop a standard and acceptable basis for reliable comparison of statistics? How to identify and then measure the impact of traditions and cultures of different countries, which might be highly relevant to their own practice but impracticable to implement, or even impossible to import into domestic arrangements?

Problems of making and utilising cross-national comparisons have been well-demonstrated in employment relations. For example, establishing a meaningful basis for comparison between Britain's strike record and that of other countries has been thwarted through differences in data collection, problems of data interpretation and in making adjustments for variations in the legal limits which circumscribe industrial disputes in different countries (Hyman 1989: 196). Faulty analysis can result in faulty diagnosis of problems, which in turn, might lead to inappropriate policy prescriptions. The disastrous 1971 Industrial Relations Act provides an example of how inadequate diagnosis can lead to misguided policy: the introduction of an approach to employer relations which owed much to the legalised American system of regulating collective behaviour failed to transplant to Britain as a consequence of its initial misreading of the state of industrial relations in Britain and its subsequent rejection by the main parties involved.

With regard to training, similar pitfalls can be contemplated: for example, whilst a reasonably common basis for estimating the quantity of training undertaken may be available, comparison of quality can be far more elusive. Even within the confines of a single country, these difficulties exist; when extended beyond national boundaries, the complexities, and scope for subsequent error, are magnified.

Despite potential difficulties, it can, nevertheless, be a fruitful exercise to sketch the broad contours of training experience found in other countries in order to provide guidelines which signal the feasible range of options for policy and practice in Britain. It might also be possible to identify common factors found in countries in a similar market position and stage of economic development which help to explain patterns of economic performance. For example, there seems to be little doubt that there is a strong positive relationship between education participation rates found in countries such as Japan and aspects of their powerful technical and economic performance (Sako and Dore 1988). Youth unemployment in Western Germany is thought to be lower, and skill acquisition higher than in Britain largely as a consequence of the 'dual' system of work and study apprenticeships and its insertion into employment policy (Prais and Wagner 1985).

The preceding chapter demonstrated that rather than adopt a policy in which the State actively helps to co-ordinate the direction of manpower, Britain has tended to rely upon promoting voluntary arrangements between employers and employees which are aimed at satisfying the immediate production needs of employers. We also saw that by maintaining the divide between education and training, public policy in

Britain has assisted in propping up the operation of the voluntarist doctrine by relegating training largely to the care of industry.

It was also pointed out that there have been occasions when the State has recognised that a voluntary approach should be tempered by State intervention. Government approaches reinforce, rather than supersede, voluntarism, as the emergent initiatives rely heavily upon the voluntary actions of the parties for the deployment and implementation of government wishes. In this way, the Industry Training Act of 1964 called for voluntary participation by industry in setting up and maintaining training boards, but even under these relatively liberal conditions the functioning of the Act was undermined by repeated calls for withdrawal of State interference from industry affairs. Similarly, the dominant influence of voluntarism helped to mould the activities and development of programmes which the MSC wished to introduce. The market relations approach adopted in the 1980s and subsequently channelled into the TECs and LECs also owes much to voluntarist thinking. With the focus on market regulation rather than planning, voluntarism could be seen as the antithesis of policy: a consequence of the hold which this tradition exerts over practice in Britain is that whenever governments have taken faltering steps simply to manoeuvre voluntarism into longer-term activities, the main parties either resist, deflect or ignore the prescriptions offered. The pervasiveness of voluntarist traditions has prevented any form of consistent centrally determined policy from taking root.

The voluntarist route for training is not one which has been followed by other countries. A typology of public policy-making has been offered by Sheldrake and Vickerstaffe whose three models are claimed to represent 'the dominant modes of funding and delivery in competitor countries' (1987: 55). The first model, termed 'free market', is based upon private funding and delivery. The United States and Japanese companies are offered as examples of this type.

The second model is termed interventionist, involving 'public funding through taxation and public organisation' with France cited as an example. Finally, there is the corporatist model with 'joint public and private funding through tripartite delivery systems within a framework of nationally agreed procedures and standards' (1987: 55). Germany is included as a representative corporatist approach largely on the basis of the level of active multi-party contribution to training decisions which has been promoted by the State for different levels of decision-making. The authors accept that their model is a simplification, shown by specifying Japanese companies, rather than Japan in their free market model, but insist nevertheless that, 'the countries linked to each model are seen as having a training culture guided practically by that particular ethos of training funding and provision' (1987: 56).

Distinctions in this typology begin to break down once educational inputs are included along with training provision as a contributor to manpower training policy. For example, as a percentage of GNP, Britain spends 4.9 per cent on education, directed largely to selective academic study, compared with the 4.4 per cent spent by the more vocationally directed, broadly participative Japanese and German educational systems (Training Statistics 1990: 117; Dore and Sako 1989: 137). Though Japan and Germany are included as different policy models, their educational funding levels and vocationally inspired objectives for education share important similarities, and contribute substantially to the subsequent quality training programmes on offer in those countries.

It may be more useful to codify training policy by widening the criteria to include education inputs, public policy toward employment relations and the employer practices which manifest themselves under different educational and policy conditions. Under such a codification France would be placed at the planned end of the spectrum, with Germany located toward the centre, Japan and America situated toward the unplanned end of the spectrum and Britain, with its voluntarist training approach, focus on market relations in employment and its limited vocational education intervention programme, fluctuating around the unplanned end.

Therefore, rather than describe practice found in each of a number of different and distinctive countries, we shall attempt to examine and compare these broad areas which singularly and together are likely to influence the extent and depth of learning acquired by people with a direct relevance for work. In this respect, we shall review educational arrangements, public policies adopted towards training and employment relations and the approaches implemented by employers toward training and development in different countries.

EDUCATIONAL PROVISION

Chapter 2 demonstrated that, at about 32 per cent, continuation rates in full-time education for 16–18-year-olds in Britain were low by international standards. Detailed comparative figures for educational and training enrolments have been provided by the *Training in Britain* study and are presented here in Table 4.1. This table starkly demonstrates major differences in enrolment rates for full-time education between

Britain and other countries. Moreover, Britain also has a higher withdrawal rate from education from age 16. In mitigation, the Report makes the point that the inclusion of part-time opportunities, apparently plentiful in Britain, 'results in some closing of the gap between UK participation rates' and those of other countries (Training Agency 1989: 66), but this ignores the essential question, as we indicated above, of quality of provision; the bulk of part-time UK provision (25 per cent of 16-year-olds and 21 per cent of 17-year-olds) has been provided by YTS, the educational value of which has been questioned both in terms of its basic objective to help 'unemployed people into jobs', rather than provide a 'scheme of education' (White 1988: 9), and the limited quality and quantity of formal qualifications associated with the programme (Jones 1988: 65).

For a number of reasons education participation rates are considered to be important; the higher the proportion of young people who proceed through education, and particularly those exposed to quantitative, analytical and linguistic disciplines, as in Japan and Germany, the greater the likelihood of building subsequent skill development and adaptability on to general principles. Hence, educational participation

Table 4.1: Education and training[1] enrolment rates for 16–17-year-olds (1988)

	Min. leaving age	Enrolment rates (%)					
		Age 16			Age 17		
		FT	*PT*	*Total*	*FT*	*PT*	*Total*
Germany[2]	15	69	31	100	43	49	92
Japan[3,4]	15	92	3	95	89	3	91
USA[5]	16–18	94	0	94	87	1	88
France[6]	16	78	9	87	68	10	78
UK[7]	16	47	37	84	32	34	66

[1] Includes apprenticeships, YTS and similar schemes.
[2] 1987; includes compulsory part-time education.
[3] Includes private sector higher education.
[4] Estimated for special training and miscellaneous schools, providing vocational training.
[5] 1986; includes private sector higher education. Minimum leaving age varies between states.
[6] 1986.
[7] Includes estimates for those studying only in the evening.
Source: Training Agency 1989: 66, table 8.1.

becomes increasingly important as the demand for unskilled work de-
clines with increased automation and the boundaries between manual
and non-manual work become blurred. In Chapter 2 we noted that whilst
expansions in the numbers of scientific and technical occupations are
anticipated, the numbers employed at the lowest skill levels are predicted to continue to fall. With educational attainments, acceptance of
change and application of technology is likely to be enhanced (Lane
1990: 253), and general skills derived from education should be widely
transferable from one task or employment context to another.

Some commentators have suggested that sustained periods of formal
education allow for ease in subsequent learning, and as new tasks are
increasingly likely to demand continuing and adaptive learning, those
who are accustomed to the learning process (who have 'learned to
learn') are again likely to be at an advantage when receiving training at
and for work, to the benefit of both employees and industry (Kenney and
Reid 1988: chapter 5). In-house training styles of large Japanese companies, which rely to a considerable extent upon independent learning,
can be implemented because of the high standards of basic education
attained by the majority of Japanese workers (Dore and Sako 1989: 80).

Further, the larger the proportion of people who continue to the
threshold of higher education, the greater the likelihood of people
passing through it, either immediately or possibly at a later stage in life.
Figures from *Training in Britain* suggest a 1986 'Higher Education New
Entrant Rate' for Britain which was comparable with Germany and
France and not far behind the USA and Japan (Training Agency 1989:
66; see also Training Statistics 1990: 116). These figures, however,
require careful interpretation; there is no standard international defi-
nition of 'higher education' and other findings have suggested that in
degree-level participation, Britain still lags seriously behind our major
trading partners. Provisional figures issued by the 1988 Labour Force
Survey indicated that only one in eight persons of working age had
qualifications above those of GCE 'A' level or their equivalent
(Training Agency 1989: 47; Cassels 1990: 42). In 1982, 22 per cent of
the relevant age group entered university in Germany, compared with 14
per cent of first-year students studying at university (8 per cent) or
polytechnic (6 per cent) in England (Prais and Wagner 1985: 180). In
1984, it was reported that 36 per cent of 18-year-olds entered higher
education in Japan compared with 14 per cent in Britain (Prais 1987:
199). Similarly, in 1986, 35 per cent of 18–19-year-olds enrolled in
higher education in the USA (DES 1989) against the apparently static 14
per cent found in Britain (DES 1989: 20).

One consequence of low participation in higher education might be a scanty flow of talented and qualified people into managerial and technical occupations. We have previously noted Handy and co-workers' findings that degree-level qualifications are poorly represented among senior managers in Britain and the training and performance consequences which may stem from this deficiency (see Chapters 2 and 5). Further, whilst there are sound economic arguments that higher education generally contributes to national economic performance (Hammermesh and Rees 1984), there is little doubt that in order to compete successfully through innovation in high technology world markets, a country requires a sound scientific, technological and engineering base (Gospel 1991: 8). In other words, a direct association between occupation, skill qualifications and performance productivity can be identified. Germany and Japan, in particular, produce scientists, engineers as well as technicians and skilled craft workers who are suited to take advantage of investment in modern technological industry. For engineering and technology, figures reproduced in Table 4.2 show that compared with France and Germany, Britain in the mid-1980s had fewer people qualifying at craft, technician and graduate levels. In 1990, EGOR, the research and consultancy group, published comparative figures for qualified engineers in major European countries. A summary of these figures is provided in Table 4.3.

Whilst Britain is producing some 18,000 qualified engineers annually, this figure is clearly not sufficient to satisfy existing requirements, with the supply of qualified graduates lagging behind current demand by some 8,000. Unfortunately, a combination of factors have helped to maintain the low profile of engineering in Britain:

> The Finniston Report (in 1981) recommended the promotion of engineering training. This advice has clearly not been followed. Indeed, the lack of incentive added to other social and cultural factors have resulted in a devaluation of the engineering professions.

Table 4.2: Numbers qualifying in engineering and technology (1985)

	UK	France	Germany
Craft	35,000	92,000	120,000
Technician	29,000	35,000	44,000
Graduate	14,000	15,000	21,000

Source: Cassels 1990: 43.

The low status on the social ladder, the attraction of the finance and accounting professions and the lack of sufficient funding have contributed to a severe shortage of engineers and technicians in the UK. To exacerbate the situation further, the next decade is set to witness a serious demographic problem.

(EGOR 1990: 61)

Converging trends of a sharp reduction in numbers of 18-year-olds and an anticipated growth of at least 20 per cent in the demand for scientific managers and related professional occupations by 1995 (EGOR 1990: 61; Ball 1990) points to an intensification of the educational problems facing technology-based industry in the UK.

A second factor which seems to be present in the more stable growth economies is the extension of education throughout the occupational range. We saw in Table 4.2 that France and Germany both produce higher numbers of craft workers and technicians than does Britain. Indeed, on the basis of their detailed investigations, Prais and Wagner maintain that major differences in 'productive quality' of the German and British labour force were attributable to the high numbers, at least 60 per cent, of the former who obtained apprenticeship or other 'intermediate-type qualifications', compared with a maximum of 30 per cent of the British labour force (1985: 175).

Table 4.3: Qualified engineers graduating annually in Europe

	Numbers qualifying (000s)	Differences between numbers qualifying and demand for qualified engineers (000s)
Germany	31	–
UK	18	8
France	14	11
Netherlands	11.2	+2.2
Spain	8.7	5.3
Italy	8.5	14.5
Belgium	4.7	4
Denmark	4	+0.8
Sweden	2.6	0.3
Portugal	2	1.5

Source: EGOR 1990: tables 1 and 3.

There is also evidence that the higher numbers of middle-ranking occupations are matched by a superior quality of educational provision than is the case in Britain. Bearing in mind the comments made above, and the quality reputations established by German and Japanese industry and the growing performance of France, it is worthwhile to consider the education systems of these countries in more depth. Above, we suggested that France represents an interventionist example for training, and this approach is clearly evident in its educational arrangements. Progressively less interventionist, but still involving a degree of central and local planning are the German and Japanese education systems. In all three cases, education participation rates, technical preparation and entrance into higher education indicate higher standards than those found in Britain.

The education system in France is organised by the State through a hierarchy of national-level qualifications. As with Germany and Japan, a high proportion (79 per cent in 1986–7) of 16-year-olds continue with their education beyond the minimum leaving age. About 64 per cent proceed to full-time Baccalauréat or less prestigious Brevet de technicien studies. The 'Bac' offers the traditional route to a university qualification, but has now been supplemented by the Baccalauréat technologique (BTn) and Baccalauréat professionnel for students wishing to undertake more practical studies. The latter has been introduced in order to help meet the French government's declared aim of having 80 per cent of the age group achieve Bac standard by the end of the decade.

Students who have acquired the vocational Brevet d'études professionnelles (BEP, approximately equivalent to the English GCSE) may now find a suitable route to continue to progress to Bac level through these courses. Lower-ability students may opt for the full-time Certificat d'aptitude professionnelle (CAP), approximately equivalent to a City and Guilds trade qualification in England, though Prais and Steedman, in their comparative study of French and British building workers, considered that the CAP offered a broader basis of practical study than its English equivalent (Prais and Steedman 1986). About 35 per cent of French pupils take either the CAP or BEP (Training Agency 1989: 68), but only a few of the CAP-qualified students are reported to progress to higher studies (Lane 1989: 70).

For occupations requiring intermediate levels of skill and qualifications there is growing evidence that the French full-time vocational educational system is proving more successful than the disjointed efforts found in Britain for comparable occupations. In French engineering firms visited by Steedman, two-thirds of shopfloor workers held at least a CAP qualification, compared with less than one in six workers with equivalent qualifications in British engineering plants (1988: 59). In craft and technical occupations, France is now approaching Germany both in quantity (as Table 4.4 demonstrates) and, following recent educational reforms outlined above, in quality also.

Similar differences in levels of qualifications were witnessed by researchers from the National Institute of Economic and Social Research (NIESR) in building trades (Prais and Steedman 1986), in office work (Steedman 1987), an especially important potential utiliser of new technology, and in the retail trades (Jarvis and Prais 1989). In all cases, superior levels of initial education have helped to give France a competitive edge over Britain.

The German secondary system of schooling is selective, with pupils attending either a Gymnasium, a Realschule or a Hauptschule. The Gymnasium is a traditionally academic institution, catering for high-ability pupils, usually to the age of 19, before they progress to university, having attained the necessary Abitur level. Realschulen are orientated to teaching scientific and technical subjects up to the leaving age of 16. Certificated students may be eligible to attend a further period of full-time study at a technical high school, which also offers certificates providing access to more advanced studies. The third type of school is the Hauptschule, which offers a certificate representing the minimum attainment level for entry into most occupations.

Table 4.5 shows in more detail the awards associated mainly with each type of school. It shows a high proportion (by English standards) of young people eligible to undertake higher education studies (28 per cent), and confirms that the vast majority of young people leave the schooling system with a formal certificated qualification at some level. Comparisons between

Table 4.4: Totals of mechanical and engineering craft and technician qualifications in three countries, 1975 and 1987

	1975			1987		
	GB (000s)	FR (000s)	GE (000s)	GB (000s)	FR (000s)	GE (000s)
Craft	16	51	78	12	68	89
Techn.	11	15	25	18	30	45

GB = Great Britain; FR = France; GE = Germany.

Source: Steedman 1988: table 6.

German qualifications and their approximate English counterparts show that the standards of the intermediate Realschulabschluss and lower level Hauptschulabschluss compare favourably with the GCE 'O' level and Certificate of Secondary Education (CSE) respectively (Prais and Wagner 1985). The German system is also typified by strong emphasis throughout on achieving satisfactory standards in a broad range of subjects. In contrast to England, certificates are not awarded for individual subjects; candidates at all levels must pass the core subjects, which include mathematics and languages, in order to qualify for completion of study certificates.

A pronounced practical orientation to the school curriculum is evident, especially at the middle and lower levels of the ability range; whilst each Land (Region or State) has the autonomy to vary its curriculum within limits set at the federal level, it is usual for Hauptschulen to introduce increasingly intensive 'work tuition' from age 13, culminating in spells of employer-based work experience in the final years of school study (Prais and Wagner 1985: 188). Career counselling is a prominent feature of the German education system which helps to guide young people toward training and occupations consistent with their aptitudes and school attainments.

Table 4.5: Types and numbers of qualifications from German schools (1982)

Certificate provided	Approx. English equivalent	School	Numbers obtained	% of Age Group
Abitur	'A' Levels	Gymnasium	210,000	21
Fachhochschulreife	'A' Levels	Vocl. upper	70,000	7
Realschulabschluss	5 'O' Levels	Realschule F/T Vocl. Gymnasium Hauptschule	240,000 80,000 40,000 60,000	34
Hauptschulabschluss	5 CSE	Realschule F/T Vocl. Gymnasium Hauptschule	290,000*	29
No certificate	–	–	100,000	9
				100

Notes: * A total of 370,000 pupils were reported as receiving this certificate in 1982, but 80,000 continued to take the higher level Realschulabschluss.

Source: Adapted from Prais and Wagner 1985: table 1.

The consequence of the depth of schooling provision and the attention given to training as a continuing and integral part of the education system is that 80 per cent of German employees achieve either academic or vocational qualifications, or both, spanning the ability range. Contrasts with Britain are only too apparent:

> Among the 400 qualifications there are some suited for low achievers at school as well as others suited for high achievers. By contrast, nearly half the British labour force has neither a vocational nor an academic qualification, and more than three-quarters is without any vocational qualifications.
>
> (Rose 1990: 24)

Subsequent training for German managers and employees can be built upon the strong educational foundations provided by the schooling system, where considerable importance is attached to numeracy, literacy and upon vocational preparation. The system encourages a high level of participation in advanced studies. We can witness similar characteristics, pursued through a different route, in another economically successful country, Japan.

School attendance in Japan is compulsory from age 6 to 15 years. During this time, children attend primary school for the first six years, followed by middle (alternatively known as lower secondary) school for three years. These schools are comprehensive, have mixed-ability classes and are free. Nearly half of lower secondary pupils, and a higher proportion in large cities, attend supplementary evening classes in their drive to gain sufficient attainments to secure entry into the highly selective high (or upper secondary) schools. At both secondary levels, mathematical problem-solving is afforded high priority; one consequence is that standards of Japanese mathematical attainment at school are reckoned to be among the highest in the world (Prais 1989: 200; Dore and Sako 1989: 6). Prais has estimated that for mathematics, Japanese children are two years ahead of English pupils by age 13, that they learn at a faster rate and that attainment variation is lower (Prais 1987: 200–1). These early achievements establish a strong platform both for subsequent education and for understanding technically intricate work.

Though compulsory schooling ends at age 15, virtually no-one withdraws from schooling at this age. On the basis of their entrance examination results, 16-year-olds are accepted either into general or vocational high schools. In 1985, 67.5 per cent of 16-year-olds entered general high school, with most then continuing with full-time studies at university (four years), junior college (two years) or special training schools (two years). Of 16-year-olds, 26.1 per cent entered vocational high school, with 2.4 per cent progressing to university or junior college, 2.3 per cent attending special training schools, and the rest (20.6 per cent) entering the labour market at age 18 (Dore and Sako 1989: 21). Thus, in contrast to Britain, we see very high educational participation rates until age 18 and a substantial proportion of young people continuing with full-time tuition beyond this age to advanced levels.

Substantive differences between Britain and Japan are also apparent. Japanese students continue with their mathematical studies at least until age 17. Also there is the division between general and vocational high schools. The general high school system provides a direct route for continued full-time academic or vocational studies (for about 70 per cent of entrants to general high schools in 1985) and subsequent developmental opportunities with major employers for most of its graduates. However, a substantial number of pupils, estimated at 1.4 million in 1984, enter vocational schools, most frequently technical (35 per cent) or commercial (40 per cent). Mechanical engineering and electrical courses are numerically the most popular subjects in the technical schools, which attract almost exclusively boys, with girls tending to go to commercial schools (Prais 1987: 206). Vocational schools are important in helping to prepare young people for middle-ranking technical positions in large firms, but especially for employment in 'the mass of technically competent small firms that are such an important feature of the Japanese industrial scene' (Prais 1987: 205). Notwithstanding their vocational orientation, these schools are expected to devote a minimum of a third of the syllabus to general education subjects such as languages and of course, mathematics, though in practice closer to a half of vocational school time is spent on general rather than specialised vocational subjects (Dore and Sako 1989: 36). There is also considerable emphasis given to theoretical aspects of the syllabus, offering opportunity for subsequent academic development.

It would seem, then, that the vocational schools play an important part in servicing the technical and commercial manpower needs of the Japanese economy. Prais calculates that allowing for size, these schools produce three times as many students with at least the equivalent of BTEC National Certificates or Diplomas in mechanical and electrical/ electronic courses, and six times as many as gain National Certificates and Diplomas in Business Studies. Excluding the lower status and less comparable Certificate 'would show the Japanese system as producing 10–20 times as many at Technical level per head of the workforce as here in the above courses' (Prais 1987: 209).

The Japanese education system does have its critics. It has been organised to contribute to an economic system whose progress is highly contingent upon technology and the means to operate and manage it. Computer literacy in industry, as shown by the opening quote in this chapter, and Japanese production emphasis on quality as the responsibility of everyone (Oliver and Wilkinson 1989) are two of its main driving forces. These trends are most pronounced in leading Japanese companies which, because of their status, career opportunities and prospects of secure employment, are eagerly sought after as potential employers among entrants to the workforce. Top companies recruit from the most prestigious universities, which in turn choose their students from the most reputable schools, into which there is intense competition for entry by young people, supported strongly by their parents. Poor early school performance can, therefore, restrict subsequent employment opportunities to the more volatile and less secure sectors of the economy.

The competitive and intensive nature of the education system which virtually introduces young people into the employment market whilst still at primary school is stressful and physically exhausting for its young participants and there are visible casualties. Equally there are bound to be numerous less visible manifestations of stress. The system is financially painful for parents, who help to pay for their children's education, with parental contributions ranging from an average 6 per cent of disposable income for children under 6 years of age to 30 per cent for young children attending a private university (Eccleston 1989: 102). Such a system openly favours the rich, with the share of undergraduates from the wealthiest fifth of households increasing from 27 per cent to 40 per cent and the share of the poorest fifth of households diminishing from 20 per cent to 12 per cent over the past twenty years (Eccleston 1989: 168).

Also obscured from view is the extent to which girls and women benefit from education (or would wish to benefit) as individuals in a society which has maintained many of its male-dominated features, for there are clear signs of inequality in education and employment. Women are strongly represented in two-year junior colleges (90 per cent women) but form only 22.6 per cent of the four-year university population. Women are also expected to withdraw from full-time work following marriage or pregnancy (Baldry 1985), and they become the first and most numerous redundant casualties of recession (Eccleston 1989: 121). In 1984, 3.28 million women, representing 22.1 per cent of the total female workforce and 70.7 per cent of total part-time employees, were working part-time. The number of female part-time employees increased four-fold since 1965. Women also account for 93 per cent of homeworkers, whose 'working conditions are generally less favourable than those of employees' (Japan Institute of Labour 1986: 14–17).

Nevertheless, it is apparent that, along with France and Germany, a higher proportion of Japanese young people are able to participate in full-time education for a greater length of time than occurs in Britain. There is also little doubt that advancement to higher education by a large proportion of young people is attributable to this high early participation rate. It also seems clear that the analytical foundations upon which general and vocational education are based help to promote workplace opportunities and effectiveness in an increasingly technological economy, a point to which we shall return when we examine employer training practice. The educational and vocational lessons for Britain from these three countries are clear:

> The urgency of raising *general* schooling attainments at early schooling ages in Britain cannot be over emphasised; a higher starting point in general subjects is necessary if vocational studies at all levels (including YTS, TVEI, BTEC) are to be pursued here as successfully as in other industrially-progressive countries.
>
> (Prais 1987: 210–11)

PUBLIC POLICY

The State exerts considerable central control over education in France. State intervention is equally apparent in the legal requirements imposed on all French companies employing ten or more people to spend a minimum of 1.2 per cent of their wage bill on training, allocated into 0.75 per cent on employee training contained in the company training plan, 0.15 per cent for training leave legally available to French employees and 0.3 per cent for programmes to promote youth employment (*European Industrial Relations Review*, September 1990: 6; Oechslin 1987: 660).

Legislation with regard to training is not confined merely to employers complying with State-determined limits; under an Act passed in 1971, companies are required to draw up annual training plans (*plans de formation*) for submission to government scrutiny. A subsequent agreement between employers and unions requires employers to consult with works committees when drawing up their training plans. Companies are required to include minutes of committee deliberations when submitting their plans to the tax authorities. Further reforms secured through joint agreement have called for the establishment of training committees in enterprises with 200 or more employees. Finally, individual training leave, available to all French employees following stipulated periods of service, is also co-ordinated nationally through a joint employer–union body.

In their comparisons between productivity and occupational and educational standards, the NIESR researchers did not examine specifically the effects of training levies imposed on employers, though other evidence suggests that its impact has been at least to expand the amounts of training provided by French industry, whose expenditure on training more than doubled in real terms from Fr 2.8 billion in 1972 to Fr 6.3 billion in 1986 (adjusted to 1972 prices, *Times Higher Education Supplement*, 15 April 1988).

The German approach to public policy exhibits numerous differences to British experience which together help to contribute toward the very different economic paths of development taken by these countries in recent years. The foundation stone of the German approach to training is the apprenticeship system and in particular the so-called dual system, whereby young people engage in a three-year apprenticeship involving practical work experience integrated with theoretical learning gained through attendance at college during this same period.

There are over 400 apprenticeships covering both craft and white-collar occupations. The Vocational Training Act of 1969 defines the occupations covered by the apprenticeships and outlines the standards, syllabus and examination requirements for each craft. The three-year course is universally recognised for its quality and consistency of standards, maintained through a system which both recognises and confirms a participative role for the principal interested parties. Each apprenticeship has a closely defined curriculum and examination procedure, with written examinations set and monitored at federal level through the National Institute for Vocational Training. Papers are marked partly at federal level with oral examinations and practical tests carried out by the local Chamber of Commerce.

The syllabus and examinations for each qualification are organised nationally by so-called 'responsible authorities', employer associations guided by training committees composed of equal numbers of employer and union representatives (*Labour Research* 1988). Changes to the curriculum are made through joint agreement secured between employers and unions. A recent example was the rationalisation of the apprenticeship programme in the metal industry, where a total of thirty-seven separate trades were reorganised into six principal activities (*Financial Times*, 25 August 1988). The participation of the union in bringing about these changes was invaluable:

> This agreement was only possible because both sides acted together. It shows that things can only happen when the unions are involved. We are not just tolerated or allowed to put forward our views, but there is real co-determination.
>
> (Head of Training, IG Metall Trade Union,
> quoted in the *Financial Times*, 25 August 1988)

Jointly policed training is also seen at the level of Chambers of Commerce and in companies. The Chamber of Commerce provides a good example of partnership. Constituted by law, membership of a Chamber of Commerce or Trade is compulsory for all firms in Germany. As an example, the Bonn Chamber of Commerce has a staff of fifty, about one-third of whom are directly involved in training, with a main responsibility to ensure that company-based training meets with the requirements of each national syllabus for the 400 qualifications. They also check that training at enterprise level is conducted by a qualified (*Meister*) trainer. The Chamber is supervised by an eighteen-strong committee composed equally of one-third employer representatives, one-third union representatives and one-third vocational teachers (*Financial Times*, 7 November 1988).

Unlike the situation in Britain, unions are fully accepted as equal partners and closely involved in training matters at plant and enterprise levels through co-determination provided by legislation passed successively in 1952, 1972 and 1976. These Acts provide for the establishment of works councils at plant level and for worker representation on supervisory boards of management and a minority presence on the management board at enterprise level. The works councils have co-determination rights (i.e. they have a legal right to be involved) over in-firm training (Lane 1989: 230). At enterprise level, in industries with parity co-determination, the effect of this participation in executive decision-making was found to ensure that 'social and employment issues became prominent in board discussion, and manpower planning and employment stability became greatly enhanced' (Lane 1989: 232).

The attractions of the apprenticeship systems are such that about 600,000 people embark upon the scheme each year, with 1.8 million participants at any one time undertaking one of the 400 occupational programmes. Though participants of apprenticeship schemes are mainly recruited from the Realschulen and Hauptschulen, some 16 per cent of the 210,000 possessors of the academic Abitur were also attracted to the apprenticeship scheme in 1984. The attraction of an occupational apprenticeship to higher-educated employees helps to demonstrate the utility of the qualification as a basis for further qualifications and advancement to Technician and high-status Meister levels and beyond (Lane 1990: 249–50).

Mobility from craft apprenticeship to executive level of management is rarely found in Britain; in 1985 only one in ten managers had a skill-based craft among their qualifications (*Financial Times*, 25 August 1988; Lane 1989: 91). A survey of nearly 700 junior and middle managers conducted for the CBI in late 1987 found that only 9 per cent had been on an apprenticeship scheme (CBI 1987).

Other differences to British practice are apparent. Training costs are formally shared between employer and State, but the low level of the apprenticeship allowance as a proportion of adult pay, estimated at between a quarter and a third (Casey 1986), suggests that apprentices, too, contribute to their 'general training'[1] to a greater extent than is found in apprenticeships in Britain, a cost factor which could act as a deterrent to employers considering taking on apprentices.

In Germany, we see a co-ordinated education and training system, with considerable emphasis given to promoting high skill content training, and with much of the responsibility for its supervision and development shared between employers and unions. Whilst the parties may differ in their priorities and how they are achieved (unions voice a concern that work-based training may become too specific or restrictive for subsequent transfer), problems are resolved through an industrial relations system which legally recognises and endorses the centrality of training to employment relations and the contribution which worker organisations can make to industrial progress. This system allows and encourages industry to adjust to the demands of advances in new technology.

If Germany provides an example of an education and employment system whose separate components are co-ordinated by the federal and Länder governments, an approach which shifts further away from formal political intervention is exemplified by Japan, seen by many as a model free-market economy, unencumbered by high state expenditure, heavy tax burdens or government-imposed instruments of regulation. Nevertheless, the State does fund a high proportion of educational provision, with public sources paying for an overall 81 per cent of all education expenditure, varying from 98.5 per cent for compulsory primary and middle schools to 81.6 per cent of high school expenditure to 53.5 per cent for universities, but contributing virtually nothing toward the private sector special training schools which catered for half a million students in 1985 (Dore and Sako 1989: 69, 137).

In economic affairs also signs of State involvement are sufficiently visible for Eccleston to regard Japan as a 'planned market economy' (1989: 88), on the grounds that the operation of market forces is somewhat more constrained than purist adherents to that doctrine might wish to acknowledge. Hence, by conveying appropriate signals to the parties involved, the 'State co-ordinates national norms for the annual spring offensive', thereby operating an informal incomes policy (1989: 91). It also devotes considerable expenditure to forms of public investment in transport systems and preparing commercial sites for company operations (1989: 94). In recession, the State has intervened in subsidising retraining and relocation costs, providing payments for early retirement and in tendering financial aid for temporary lay-offs (1989: 121). All this amounts to 'a supportive environment that has provided the base for economic expansion' (1989: 106). One consequence has been rates of official unemployment, which at around a constant 2 per cent, have been the envy of many Western economies during the crisis years of the 1980s (Japan Institute of Labour 1990: table 20).

EMPLOYER TRAINING PRACTICE

An inverse relationship might be expected between high state involvement in vocational education and training and the amounts of training provided by employers. In other words, comprehensive centralised planning and intervention policies are not thought to be conducive to high employer training activity, and the lower planned, market-based approach is more inclined to stimulate training by and through industry. To some extent, this relationship holds good; Japanese companies, for example, operating in a relatively free market environment, have secured a positive reputation for training provision. On the other hand, Britain, which subscribes to a voluntary code based on market forces, provides little. At the planned end of the continuum as well, evidence suggests that French companies are prepared to go beyond the minimal requirements conferred by their legislation. It appears that other influences must be important in encouraging employer training participation.

Notwithstanding the legislative requirement that French companies appropriate 1.2 per cent of their wage costs to training, which might be expected to provide a barrier to additional outlays, actual expenditure on training is higher, averaging 2.74 per cent overall (*European Industrial Relations Review*, September 1990: 6). Levels of 3.62 per cent have been reported for companies with over 2,000 employees, 4 per cent in petrochemicals and as high as 7 per cent for the gas and electricity companies. Along with transport, where average training expenditure is also high (5.80 per cent of wage bill in enterprises employing more than 2,000 employees in 1983), gas and electricity are part of the public sector where through high union density, it is likely that 'more pressure to train is brought to bear through the works committees when discussing the training plans' (Handy *et al.* 1988: 106). Levels of expenditure in excess of 10 per cent of wage bills have been reported for some highly technological companies. Even small companies with between 10 and 19 employees train more than is required by the legal minimum (Oechslin 1987: 660; *Labour Research* 1988: 12; *Times Higher Education Supplement*, 15 April 1988).

There is also evidence that industries and companies have been stimulated by the legislation to embark upon collaborative initiatives in their training activities. Small and medium-sized enterprises possess limited facilities to offer their own training and, in consequence, many of their employer associations have established training associations to advise on, assist with and deliver training to small and medium-sized concerns. The governing bodies of these associations are assisted by joint training committees composed of employer and union signatories to the relative agreements (Oechslin 1987: 660).

Companies may also have become inspired to inject a more participative element into their relationships with unions at enterprise level, a locus where union involvement has traditionally been strongly resisted by French management. A useful example is offered by Renault, who, following several years of fraught relationships with its unions, has now entered into a new negotiated agreement and a new spirit of collaboration with 'a progressive policy for the individual and collective management of human resources in order to ensure the success of Renault and contribute actively to the professional, personal and cultural development of its employees' (*European Industrial Relations Review*, March 1990). The company's wide-ranging strategy for its future development is especially noteworthy for management's willingness to involve unions at company and plant level and for the centrality given to training as an instrument of major change in the agreement.

Despite these advances, there is no doubt that problems still persist in the French industrial skills structure. An absence of continuity between full-time vocational education and workplace development is compounded by a lack of vertical integration between vocational qualifications; together these constraints have acted as a barrier over which it is difficult for employees to climb toward further development. One consequence is that junior management is under-developed relative to Germany, where '70.2 per cent of foremen have a qualification above the *Facharbeiterbrief* (apprenticeship completion certificate), in France only 11 per cent have a training above the CAP, and 50 per cent have no training at all' (Lane 1989: 77).

Rigidity is further exacerbated through the rather inflexible promotion system found in France, with mobility based upon a combination of conduct and seniority, the low take-up of individual training leave (possibly because it requires employer consent, which is not always easy to obtain; see Handy *et al.* 1988: 116) and the tendency for management, technical workers and men generally to gain most benefit from the employer training levy at the expense of lesser skilled manual workers. Figures released by the government show that only 11 per cent of the latter benefit from training as opposed to about one-third of male technician/management grades (Handy *et al.* 1988: 106 and table 4.9; Lane 1989: 75). Some of these problems may be addressed through the new apprenticeship system, which has been modelled on the German 'dual approach', where legislation provides for work-based apprenticeships to cover a wide range of occupations and to provide opportunity for advancement through progressive skill qualifications.

In Germany, the education system, legal requirements for craft training and recognition of a 'social partnership' between employers and unions which allows scope for union involvement in monitoring and regulating training, provide a solid base upon which employers can extend training beyond the initial requirements demanded of them. The law also determines who can undertake or supervise training in the form of the *Meister*, a skilled worker who has gained additional practical and theoretical qualifications. Over 2 million workers have achieved this qualification (Rose 1990: 21). Beyond these restrictions, further enterprise-based training is not regulated by formal institutions, but 'is nevertheless well established and widely practiced' (Lane 1990: 249).

There is no single reason which explains this approach; rather a number of factors are interwoven within the fabric of German industrial policy and employment practice. In particular, industry has consciously adopted a high technology, high skill strategy, in pursuit of which it has been supported by government policy and by the long-term benefits anticipated through close association between industry and financial institutions. As a consequence, investments in technology and in people have become central to management philosophy as well as practice:

> Training is not merely seen as an extra cost, as it is mostly regarded in Britain, but as a worthwhile and indeed, indispensable investment which is as important as investment in technology.
>
> (Lane 1990: 250)

Human investment is complemented by a career structure which encourages people, through pay rewards and potential for mobility, to supplement additional qualifications to the solid base provided by the education system. It is no accident that large company training efforts are directed most at junior and then middle managers rather than their senior colleagues (Handy *et al*. 1988: 143). Together these diverse strands, reinforced through moral and financial support from government, have helped to shape a distinct managerial strategy in which training takes a central part and the role of the Meister trainer becomes crucial:

> A Meister normally has status, authority and higher pay vis-a-vis fellow workers, and is able to deal with both management and the shopfloor. The adult front-line supervisor of a youth in training is not segregated from normal production workers and categorised (or stigmatised) as an instructor, as is often the case in Britain.
>
> (Rose 1990: 21)

The cumulative effects of these policies and strategies on the performance of German industry have been fully explored in a range of comparative studies undertaken by the National Institute of Economic and Social Research. The findings, which help to confirm the growing technological and skill disadvantages under which British industry labours, are considered in greater depth in Chapter 5.

Whilst public policy in France and to a lesser extent, Germany, adopts a high profile role, in Japan the State provides a passive supportive environment within which companies are able to conduct their affairs. Set against this benign context, the main source for subsequent development of manpower in Japan comes from employers.

Among modern economies, Japan is probably, with its unique traditions, the most difficult to emulate. These difficulties have not prevented some British companies from attempting to adopt those elements of the Japanese system which appear at any time to provide ready-made solutions to their problems, such as the introduction of quality circles, but then wondering why no apparent difference in employee performance has resulted (see Oliver and Wilkinson 1989). The truth is that large Japanese companies and public sector employers, which together employ about 19 per cent of the Japanese labour force, subscribe to clear-cut philosophies in which their employment practices are deeply embedded. Even among these companies, however, not all employees are embraced by the community corporate philosophy. Part-timers and temporary workers, who together comprise 11 per cent of the labour force, are excluded.

Of greatest significance from the point of view of this book is the practice of life-time employment which large companies provide for their key employees. In return, the company looks for and expects a high degree of loyalty from its life-time staff. The relations and mutual obligations which are forged between the parties resemble those of 'family' or at least, of community. There are a number of practical implications which emerge from this approach. First, companies recruit their staff on the expectation that, once appointed (a) employees will stay with the company and (b) that the company will retain the services of the employee. Recruitment is then conducted for career rather than occupational purposes, and, especially with university recruits, a good academic record allied to desirable personal qualities will form major criteria for selection, and not necessarily the course of study undertaken (Sako and Dore 1988: 77).

These mutual obligations underline the salience of training within the Japanese enterprise. Training is essential to the employer because virtually all Japanese companies recruit their employees 'as green untrained labour' (Baldry 1985) directly from the education system. To be of value to the Japanese enterprise, the recruits must first be trained. For this reason, the bulk of identifiable training occurs during the early part of the employee's tenure (Handy et al. 1988: 32; Dore and Sako 1989: 87). Nevertheless, the employer who makes a 'commitment' to employ for life may also require to train or retrain employees for diversification into new occupational areas if current commercial activities become threatened.

From the perspective of employees, life-time employment demands loyalty and commitment from them and many are prepared to undertake training in order to perform their existing tasks better or to meet employer needs for qualified labour.[2] As Dore and Sako point out, in such an environment, where training or retraining is an established feature of employment activity, all grades of permanent employees are expected both to learn and to teach; the organisation is very much a 'learning organisation' (1989: 79).

With employees learning from one another and teaching each other (a facet which is encouraged by performance appraisal systems which offer advancement and reward to managers whose own subordinates have made progress within the organisation), much of the training which takes place is informal and specific to the company, often built up through informal manuals written by managers and supervisors for their staffs. Highly literate and numerate employees would be expected to cope with and benefit from this rather unstructured approach to workplace learning. This learning environment is reinforced by other personnel practices which encourage employee participation, such as job rotation and quality circles, which within Japanese companies are not stitched on to an otherwise unchanged organisational structure, but are part of a unified management process.

In the light of the foregoing it is not too surprising that attempts to quantify the amounts of training provided by Japanese enterprises have revealed apparently low levels of expenditure. Figures suggest that in companies with thirty or more employees, annual budgeted training expenditure in manufacturing industry amounts to no more than £60 per employee! As a percentage of the wage bill manufacturing enterprises employing more than 5,000 employees spent 0.5 per cent on budgeted training in 1984, compared with 0.1 per cent in firms with less than 100 workers (Chingin 1984, reported in Dore and Sako 1989: 80–81). Bearing in mind our earlier comments about Japanese management philosophy and practice which treats training as an integral part of enterprise practice it can be seen that these figures should be treated with extreme caution, particularly if compared to a British experience dominated by insecurity for employees and lack of participative practice in training.

An additional aspect of the loyalty equation is the willingness of Japanese employees to undertake external courses which help them in the execution of current tasks. Many of these courses are undertaken by employees largely or totally in their own time, but with possible financial assistance from employers. Following the 1984 Vocational Training Act, employers who provide assistance to employees can apply to the government for a subsidy which covers a proportion of the course costs. About 1,200 courses, validated by the Education Ministry, are eligible for subsidy.

The above practices relate to larger establishments, employing 1,000 employees or more, very much a minority of the nation's workforce. A much higher proportion of the employed labour force, about 70 per cent, work in establishments employing less than 1,000 employees. In 1986, over three-quarters of employees in the private sector were found in establishments employing less than 100 people; 68 per cent of all establishments, employing a total of 19 per cent of the private sector workforce, employed not more than four people (Japan Institute of Labour 1990: table 13). Do these smaller enterprises offer any significant differences in training practice?

On a per capita basis, training budget expenditures in manufacturing companies employing less than 100 employees are about a fifth of those in large enterprises employing more than 5,000 employees, a pattern which conforms to other countries, but bearing in mind Japanese management philosophy and enterprise practice, is not necessarily a meaningful statistic. According to Eccleston, pressures of work intensification in small companies are greater even than in the larger ones, but with little or no compensatory security of tenure (1989: 68–9). With external labour market considerations greater for small companies, it comes as no surprise that 'small employers are more likely to look to the external market for the skills they need as an alternative to doing their own training' (Dore and Sako 1989: 110). Nevertheless, the same authors point to a survey that shows that half of companies with between 30 and 99 employees 'did have somebody specifically responsible for training'. Training in small companies is also less development-centred and more reliant upon external sources for its provision (1989: 111).

SUMMARY AND CONCLUSIONS

This chapter has presented a number of influences which bear upon training provision in different countries. The areas examined – education, relations of employment and employer policies and practice – were chosen for their relative permanence and because each area has a clear relationship with learning and with developing appropriate skill and work capabilities.

A fully comprehensive comparative study would require an examination of the contributions made by other features of State policy to performance productivity: for example, little attention has been given to broad economic policy, regional policies or to wider employment subsidy programmes, though these can undoubtedly influence training provision and work performance. Nevertheless, the main intention has been to concentrate on those long-standing policy features which over time are most likely to influence learning and work performance and which might have most relevance for domestic application.

With regard to education, considerable State interest and involvement was evident even in nominally 'market economies' such as Japan. A feature common to all the countries examined is the extent of post-compulsory continuation in full-time education and high participation rates in advanced education. As a consequence, high numbers of people are initially qualified to enter into and train for the technical, scientific and managerial occupations demanded by fast-developing industries.

One of the themes explored in this book is the extent to which training is encouraged by the State as an integral feature of employment relations, whether through legislation or by governmental example. Both in France and Germany we found evidence of State intervention through the legal requirement for the involvement of Works Councils in enterprise training plans. In Japan, management philosophy and practice extensively embraces employee training within employment relations in a high-growth economic environment promoted by the State. Even in an interventionist country like France, where the State prescribes minimum training levels, companies tend to train above the levels legally required of them; it appears that the legislation, rather than deterring supplementary training, can act as a stimulus. Employers in Germany and Japan build upon strong learning platforms provided by education as a basis for substantial and continuing in-work development without State compulsion.

Finally, we need to consider what lessons, if any, can be applied to Britain from overseas experience. Chapter 2 showed that steps were being taken to remedy the abysmal education participation rate for post-compulsory and higher education. It is to be hoped that these initiatives bear fruit, because it is apparent that other countries are increasing their educational efforts beyond the levels currently in force. Britain therefore needs to do more and to do it more quickly merely in order to maintain the existing educational distance and to prevent it from becoming an unbridgeable chasm.

We also have seen that in public employment relations policy, traditional voluntarist principles are not merely being upheld, but reinforced through such moves as the abolition of the MSC, reducing the numbers of Training Boards and restricting their powers and subsequently through passing responsibility for local training to TECs and LECs. Collective influence on employment relations has been diminished through a series of measures aimed at curtailing union influence over employment relations whilst market competition for labour has been further encouraged by stripping away protective legislation for individual employees.

In Britain, the government has strengthened its reliance upon exhortation to employers to train and to employees to get trained as part of its low intervention market-led beliefs. As seen with Japan, such a detached approach to training can succeed but it requires employers to adopt employment policies and practices consistent with high training investment. The second half of this book explores the ways in which employers in Britain are responding to this challenge.

Chapter 5

Training provision in Britain

> Above all, we must invest in the skills and knowledge of our people and build up industry's skill base, through a strategy of training through life, to enable Britain to continue to grow and to generate jobs. *The prime responsibility for this investment lies with employers.*
>
> (Employment for the 1990s 1988, emphasis added)

INTRODUCTION

A major feature of a market competition orientation to economic policy is an assumption of rational economic decisions made by individual worker sellers and individual employer buyers based upon reliable information circulated between the parties. Hence, labour will only attempt to acquire those skills clearly in demand. Similarly, employers will be encouraged to train their employees if the benefits to them appear to be worthwhile. For employers, the broader long-term aspirations of government policy (of 'investing in the skills and knowledge of our people' and providing 'training through life') may be of little relevance. Our quote from the personnel representative in Chapter 3 showed explicitly that employers expect to achieve commercial objectives; they should not be expected to act as government agents (see p. 52). Under these conditions, employers might be prepared to train for immediate or clearly perceived manpower requirements; though equally, they might not train, of course. Buying in the outcomes of other employers' training efforts remains a viable alternative under free-market criteria. Other options, such as operating at a low skill level are also available (Training Agency 1989: 41). Employers might be slow to appreciate that their individual failure to train may also be harmful to their longer-term interests.

Government responsibility under the voluntarist method is limited to its service as a catalytic agent for facilitating smooth co-ordination between the component parts of the economic system. The role of government is to offer: 'information provision, encouragement of training standards, setting-up pump-priming courses in new technologies and provision of training assistance to the unemployed and disabled' (IMS 1984, quoted in Keep 1989: 196). This shows that although under market conditions government intervention in economic affairs is restricted, voluntarism does not relegate the State to act as a mere bystander to the operation of market forces; it is after all answerable to the electorate for economic progress and acknowledges that in a complex society, automatic or instantaneous adjustments between different demands and expectations of consumers, producers and factors of production occur neither automatically nor instantaneously. One strand to voluntarist government policy has been therefore, to provide information which allows participants and potential participants to recognise and act upon existing surpluses and shortfalls in manpower requirements.[1] A second strand is to offer an information service which aims to alert employers to anticipated manpower needs and where possible to induce them to make appropriate provision for the future. Though this encouragement takes different forms, it relies primarily upon exhortation on the basis of prophesying dire consequences for companies in terms of commercial failure if the proffered advice is not acted upon. The repeated doom-laden warnings made to industry with regard to current demographic trends and the implications of the 1992 Single European Market are obvious demonstrations of this approach.

A dominant theme to this informational service has been to contrast and publicise domestic economic performance with that of competitor countries and to indicate the reasons for shortcomings on the UK side. Other initiatives have been to undertake various audits of employer training performance and to assess the extent of change over time. A third approach complements the first two and signals to employers the major changes and threats which they can anticipate in the future to serve as a stimulus for action. The government body most involved in this information dissemination and early warning service has been, until its recent abolition, the Manpower Services Commission. Throughout the 1980s, the MSC issued or commissioned a series of reports and studies designed to highlight employer training practice, deficiencies in its provision, competitor policy and the implications for employers of impending manpower and broader changes. Report findings were used as a lever to encourage employers to plan methodically for the future, to train systematically, and to combine the two by treating training as an integral feature of planned corporate strategy (see Ainley and Corney 1990).

EMPLOYER TRAINING PRACTICE

A variety of published reports have attempted to identify the extent and depth of employer commitment to training and a number of these can be highlighted. One study, sponsored jointly by the MSC and the National Economic Development Office (NEDO), compared standards of training and vocational education in Britain with Japan, West Germany and the USA (IMS 1984). With the exception of Britain, in all these countries vocational education is afforded high priority, not least by employers. An additional criticism directed at Britain in this report was the lack of information collection, analysis and dissemination undertaken with regard to training and associated activities. Further studies were commissioned in order to remedy this informational deficiency and to act as catalyst to encourage greater attention to training matters, especially by employers, at whom the bulk of studies were especially directed.

A Challenge to Complacency (1985)

This study, conducted by the consultants Coopers & Lybrand, was published under its ominous title but with the sub-titled aspiration of *Changing Attitudes to Training* (1985). The research comprised four main components: interviews with senior representatives from sixty companies, examination of forms of training provision, financial and tax aspects of training provision and a brief review of overseas experience.

With regard to employer training activities, the findings were as depressing as the title suggests, leading the researchers to conclude that: 'Few employers think training sufficiently central to their business for it to be a main component in their corporate strategy; the great majority did not see it as an issue of major importance' (1985: 4). Reasons for this detached approach derived largely from the complacency of senior managers, compounded by ignorance of their own companies' performance in training matters or the level of resources committed to training. Specifically, few executives saw any direct input from training into profits; conversely, many saw training as an outcome of healthy profits rather than as a major contributor to them. The researchers also found that a context of 'environmental uncertainty' was likely to act as a training deterrent. As uncertainty is a central feature of a market economy, this raises considerable doubts as to whether, in the absence of external support, a self-regulating market system is likely to produce the levels of skills and abilities needed in response to a changing commercial climate. This point gathers strength when company managers contended that there were few external pressures, including government actions, exerted upon companies to train; this was in stark contrast to other countries which enjoyed a 'strong cultural pressure or a clear legislative structure', or both, for companies to train (1985: 5).

Senior managers' views which located training in such insignificant terms were reflected in company practice: training was seen as an overhead cost and largely delegated to line managers. There was little analysis of training needs or evaluation of training efforts. Training specialists tended to have low managerial status. The study concluded with the warning that major changes in employer attitudes were required as well as a more supportive environment for them to make training and manpower decisions.

The dominant and worrying theme pervading the Coopers & Lybrand study concerned attitudes expressed by senior management. Concern at UK management performance is not new: the Royal Commission on Trade Unions and Employers Associations (Donovan) Report of 1968 had some harsh words to say about the standards of management at establishment level, stimulating increasing research interest into the behaviour of managers, their responsibilities and the ways in which these are discharged. Moreover, a series of projects undertaken in the 1960s and 1970s which examined the extent and nature of training provision for managers in Britain were largely critical of the low numbers of managers undergoing recognised formal programmes of development and questioned the relevance of these programmes to manager or employer needs. Nevertheless, despite the breadth and depth of criticism, little action was taken by companies (see Sadler 1989).

For a number of reasons the 1980s saw a resurgence in interest in managerial behaviour. Intensified competition within the market economy places considerable responsibility upon managers to make decisions quickly and efficiently; incompetent decisions lead to corporate failure which, ultimately, contributes to national economic decline. Moreover, managers of successful organisations in the world's leading economies appear to be highly educated and beneficiaries of a well-developed training system, indicating a strong positive link between education, training, management proficiency and organisational performance (Handy *et al*. 1988).

An additional reason for interest was that government policies had served to restrict the influence of trade unions, which in association with the competitive product climate, placed greater emphasis on the need for employers to manage with the willing co-operation of employees. The apparent inefficiency of confrontational workplace relationships and the increasing legal restrictions imposed upon unions led to closer evaluation of management styles and techniques capable of commanding individual employee commitment and the spawning of a mass of new research and literature on management strategies both in Britain and elsewhere (see Kochan *et al*. 1986, Purcell 1987: Marginson *et al*. 1988). The seminal work of Peters and Waterman (1982) in helping to define the corporate qualities which lead to organisational 'excellence' has been a major factor in stimulating this renewed interest.

Third, as we have seen, reports such as that by Coopers & Lybrand above were highly critical of senior management apathy; attention started to be given to the ways in which management might be steered in more positive directions. A company headed by executives, themselves educated and trained, would be likely to promulgate these same qualities in their staff; organisations could become 'learning organisations', with the example set from the top.

Finally, doubts about the relevance and value of existing programmes of training and education on offer to managers or potential managers had circulated for a number of years (NEDC 1963; Mant 1969). The essence of these criticisms was the perceived distance between academically dominated formal programmes of instruction for managers and the practical tasks performed by them; management education was seen as a waste of time and in consequence not greatly used by employers. These studies emerged at a time when psychologists were beginning to investigate and report on new approaches to management learning. In particular, the 'learning cycle' introduced by Kolb *et al*. (1974), in which work experience acts as a source of learning, experimentation and potential performance improvement, kindled considerable interest in applying theories of learning to management effectiveness and advancement. These ideas were later developed and operationalised by Mumford in his categorisation of contextual learning styles (Mumford 1987). Ramifications of both areas of study can be found in the recent emphasis on 'experiential' learning (i.e. learning through experience) as a prime source of management development.[2]

Handy and Constable and McCormick reports (1987)

The concerns discussed above led to the commissioning of two complementary studies, one examining demand and supply of management
training and education, and ways in which these could be matched, and
the other looking at the state of British management education and
development in comparison with competitor countries.

The two reports were published jointly in 1987. '*The Making of
British Managers*', prepared by Constable and McCormick, was sponsored by two government departments, with support from the CBI and
British Institute of Management. The study included an interview
survey conducted in the autumn of 1986 with representatives from 206
major public and private sector organisations. The report estimates a
total of between 2.5 and 3 million employees with managerial responsibilities in the UK, supplemented by about 90,000 new entrants into the
ranks of management each year. The vast majority of existing and
emerging managers have no previous management education and only a
small number receive subsequent opportunities for work-based development. The average training period for managers amounts to one day
annually.

An earlier survey of British managerial experience produced consistently unfavourable findings, observing that over half of all firms failed
to make formal training provision for their managers. Even among firms
with over 1,000 employees, a fifth were failing to train (Mangham and
Silver 1986). Though the Constable and McCormick survey findings
were somewhat more favourable, with 85 per cent of the organisations
claiming to have 'explicit management development policies' (Constable
and McCormick 1987, reproduced in Handy *et al.*, 1988: 186), the
researchers expressed doubts as to the degree of comprehensiveness of
policy. We could add that formal personnel policy is not necessarily
translated into consistent action. As Brewster and his colleagues have
pointed out, a formal or espoused company personnel policy may well be
superseded in practice by more prestigious or pressing production or
financial requirements, leading managers to operationalise these senior
management priorities at the expense of lower priority personnel issues
(1981). The dubious status of training and development in the eyes of
senior management would seem to mark training/development policies
as candidates for operational relegation in the priority stakes, though their
'policy' status might remain formally intact.

Nevertheless, four-fifths of the survey respondents had a training
budget, varying from a minimum annual direct training expenditure of

£100 to a maximum of £1,000 (mean £482) for each manager. Mean aggregate expenditure for developing individual managers was estimated at approximately £877 a year, comparing favourably with the earlier estimate of £600 in the Mangham and Silver study.

Unfortunately, any optimism engendered by this last finding is soon dispelled by the results of the Handy study, sponsored by the National Economic Development Council and British Institute of Management in association with the MSC. The report, presented in two parts, was later revised for publication in book form in 1988. Examining the education and development processes for managers in four competitor countries, Handy and his colleagues were forced to concede that:

'Britain does not bother much about the education and development of her managers, relying instead on a Darwinian belief in the emergence of the strongest and the best' (Handy *et al.* 1988: 178).

This conclusion was arrived at through an examination of the management education and training practices and philosophies of the different countries. Whilst clear variations emerge, it became apparent that each country, in its own way, was prepared to commit resources to management that Britain was far less inclined to do. Handy reports that in the United States, as a reflection of the status of managerial careers, a 'quarter of all undergraduates . . . are majoring in business studies and one quarter of all postgraduate students are studying for an MBA' (1988: 5); 85 per cent of top managers in America possess a degree. American corporations lend vigorous support to development, with major corporations spending about 1.6 per cent of their turnover on workforce training, equivalent to about $2,000 per employee a year (1988: 60). No doubt, expenditure on manager training would comfortably exceed this sum. Nearly half of the top 300 companies offer at least five days of off-the-job training a year to their managers.

In Japan, a different ethos prevails; business studies are not highly developed as a subject for academic or practical study. Rather, a high standard of general education is seen as the essential prerequisite for a managerial career. Again, a great majority of senior Japanese executives are educated up to graduate level (85 per cent) or beyond. Once recruited to an organisation, personal development integrates with a personnel philosophy geared to retain and progress managers in the organisation throughout their productive lives (see Chapter 4).

Two-thirds of top French managers hold a degree, but work-based training is maintained by a training tax which ensures that a minimum 1.2 per cent of the gross wage bill for any company with more than ten employees is directed to employee training. As was shown earlier, many companies spend in excess of this minimum requirement; and companies with 2,000 or more staff were estimated to spend three times this amount on training (1988: 2). It has been estimated that about one-third of training expenditure is allocated to manager training (1988: 106).

The (West) German system is typified by the high regard given to education, especially of technical subjects, throughout the managerial hierarchy, where professional expert authority is seen as the appropriate basis for corporate custodianship. Consequently, management is perceived in strictly functional, as opposed to generalist, terms. Two-thirds of managing directors hold a degree standard diploma, and in some industries 'the doctor title is almost essential for the upper ranks of management' (1988: 134). In 1984, more than half of 'first' level management held a university level diploma, a considerable increase from the 36 per cent holding this qualification ten years earlier.

In Germany, commitment to management development increases with company size, tends to be focused on less senior levels of management and is usually internally resourced, probably as a result of the concentration of manpower development in larger concerns with established internal training facilities. Technical advancement tends to dominate the development programme. Problems arising from the German system are that the functional approach to education and development leaves little room for occupational mobility, compounded in geographical terms by a reluctance for German workers to re-locate. Also, women are heavily under-represented in managerial positions owing to a combination of masculine prejudice, tradition and absence of support mechanisms (1988: 149–52).

Though different approaches were adopted among the four countries to management development a number of common features were noted in the report. These were that large companies tend to be the front-runners in management development and that company policies, procedures and practice reflect the esteem attached to training and development; high proportions of young people enter post-compulsory education, establishing a sizeable pool of potential managerial talent. In consequence, the majority of senior managers in these countries possess degree-level qualifications. Recognising that the need for specialist skills is likely to extend down and through organisations, competitor countries are planning for ever more qualified personnel to take on managerial responsibilities: 'Business and management education will become an almost universal requirement as the whole workforce becomes more skilled and more autonomous' (1988: 11).

Unfortunately, very few of these positive trends were identified in Britain, where, the authors contend, management is undertaken as a practical art rather than as an applied science. Managerial selection and promotion is dominated by rewarding vaguely martially derived virtues such as character, initiative, imagination and energy. The consequence is that only one-quarter of top British managers are educated to degree level, and that 'no clear pathway to a managerial career nor a clear philosophy of how management can best be taught, or learnt or developed' has become established (1988: 164). Too few people have been educated for management, and with the exception of a minority of committed employers, few managers receive subsequent training or opportunities for development.

As intended, these two studies excited considerable consternation among management circles, leading to the formation of the Council for Management Education and Development (CMED), which laid down a Management Charter of good training practice, inviting employing organisations to subscribe. By October 1989, some 350 employers, representing 6.5 million employees, had signed up to follow the Code of Practice. The Code simply requires 'commitment' by companies to develop their managers and provides for no monitoring of practice. Many leading companies already operating along the lines of the Code have been signatories. Together, these factors do not make for an easy assessment of the Charter's impact. On the other hand, the expansion of business qualifications was unequivocally given a boost by the reports, leading many higher education institutions to introduce introductory Certificates and intermediate Diplomas in Business Administration to lead to the prime MBA qualification, and to offer wider access to business students through open learning and in-house MBAs. It appears that some foundations for change in the practices of British management have been laid by the reports and through the subsequent publicity given to them.

Training in Britain (1989)

The most comprehensive aggregate source for data on employer training activity is provided by the 1989 report, *Training in Britain*, prepared by the Training Agency. The report arose from a survey, conducted in 1986 and 1987, covering 1,500 establishments, and supplemented by head office contact with 140 organisations. Approximately 80 per cent of the employed workforce were covered by the surveyed organisations. Case studies and interviews were also undertaken as part of the project.

Overall national expenditure on training was calculated at £33 billion annually, representing approximately 8 per cent of GDP and equivalent to 7 per cent of total man [sic] years worked. Employer contributions to training expenditure amounted to £18 billion or 54.5 per cent of total national expenditure. Employers claimed to provide training for 48 per cent of their employees. One employer in five provided no training at all with lack of training especially common in construction (30 per cent of employers provided no training), wholesale/transport (30 per cent) and manufacturing processing (27 per cent). In contrast, all employers in 'extraction/energy' and 'central and local government' provided training. The public sector provided more days of training per employee (9.0) than private sector services (6.6) or private manufacturing (5.4).

For employees receiving training, the number of training days amounted on average to 14.5 during the year, with apprentices and long-term trainees such as nurses receiving the most and established employees the least (1989: 12). Training was widespread in health (78 per cent of employees trained), retail (68 per cent), extraction/energy (64 per cent) and education (64 per cent), but in terms of numbers of days training received by employees, workers in construction with an average of 23.8 days, health (22.5) and engineering (electrical 18.2; mechanical 17.7) were the prime beneficiaries.

Approximate comparisons made with earlier reports suggest 'a significant increase (in employer training activity) over the last few years' (1989: 13) chiefly through extending coverage of training in existing 'training' companies. The likelihood of a company providing training grew substantially with size: a quarter of establishments with 10–24 employees failed to provide any training, narrowing to 10 per cent for establishments with 50–99 employees, but less than 4 per cent of establishments with more than 200 employees failed to train (1989: 37–8). Interestingly, in smaller organisations which did train, little difference in the proportions of employees receiving training, or in number of days provided, was found compared with larger establishments.

Improving competitiveness was the most frequently cited single factor influencing employers to train, cited by 56 per cent of training employers. Nevertheless, government action, both direct and indirect, exerts a surprisingly high effect. Thirty-six per cent of training establishments said that legislation was an influence, especially in manufacturing, where a half of respondents referred to legislation. YTS and other government programmes were mentioned by nearly one-third of establishments and 12 per cent referred to government-sponsored Industry Training Boards (1989: 41–2). A preliminary conclusion from these findings is that government action can stimulate companies to provide training for employees and potential entrants into the workforce. Among non-training establishments, slightly more than half claimed to have a static or declining workforce, already trained. Over 40 per cent recruited people with prior experience, suggesting at least an element of companies' benefiting from previous training. No mention was made by employers of resistance from trade unions to training proposals made by management as a training deterrent.

We mentioned above that market regulation is likely to lead to attempted satisfaction of employer short-term labour and skill requirements, and indeed, the study appears to confirm this tendency: 'decisions on training are usually taken as a response to immediate pressures. There is little evidence of longer-term investment horizons playing a significant role in employers' outlook' (1989: 43).

Costs and benefit evaluations were rarely undertaken and only a minority of trainers (30 per cent) had any systematic plans for training. Internal politics appears to be a major determinant of the training stance taken by companies and in this respect: 'the views of senior management and the chief executive in particular are very important' (1989: 43). It appears that in the mid-1980s, attitudes of senior management toward training provision were little altered from those identified in the 'complacency' days of the early 1980s.

In an associated survey based on interviews conducted with 2,500 people, the researchers also canvassed the views of individuals with regard to their training experiences. Wide differences in training provision were reported. Two-thirds of economically active individuals aged 19–59 claimed not to have received any formal training over the previous three years. However, when training is provided, young people, those with higher educational and skill qualifications and previous recipients of training appear to be the prime beneficiaries. A high proportion of individuals had few expectations of receiving any training or intentions to seek it in the future. The interviews with individuals helped to confirm the short-term nature of most training provided by employers which 'was reported usually to be of short duration and focused on the immediate needs of the job' (1989: 11).

The National Institute of Economic and Social Research (NIESR) Studies

Findings from the above general studies are supported by results from a series of detailed research projects conducted by the National Institute of Economic and Social Research. International productivity comparisons form the central focus of these studies, which take both a macro and micro perspective of the contribution of vocational education and training to economic performance. The macro-studies are based on an examination of the systems of vocational education established and practised in Germany, Japan and France. The conclusions reached with regard to Britain are familiar: *general* standards of education must be improved and broadened as a foundation for vocational education and training, especially for the middle and lower ability ranges who are particularly poorly catered for in the present British education system (Prais and Wagner 1985; Prais 1987; NIESR 1989).

The micro-level studies involve attempts to measure the contribution of training to performance at plant level. Samples of plants in Britain and West Germany, matched for size and product, were examined in metal working (Daly *et al.* 1985), kitchen furniture (Steedman and Wagner 1987), clothing (Steedman and Wagner 1989) and hotels (Prais *et al.* 1989). In all the industries studied, the higher calibre of the German worker, and in particular, of the manager, was apparent. With respect to the plants manufacturing kitchen furniture, the researchers concluded that, despite access to the same technology:

> the qualifications of those employed were entirely different. Nine-tenths of all German employees had vocational qualifications based on a three year apprenticeship type course; in Britain only one-tenth came near to being in that category.
>
> (Steedman and Wagner, 1987, in NIESR 1989: 131)

The educated workers in Germany formed the basis for future qualified supervisory and management staff. Differences in manpower quality were reflected in a productivity differential of 50–60 per cent, higher standards of output and greater flexibility in production. In addition to the fundamental educational differences which separate the German from British workforce, greater commitment to workplace training by German employers was apparent:

> German foremen and management spent much time selecting operators for retraining for CNC technology: such retraining extended from two weeks to six months. In Britain, 'a few days' retraining was

often regarded as adequate to equip an operator for new CNC machinery.

(Steedman and Wagner 1987)

One important consequence of initial high-standard practical qualifications is that it avoids costly and time-consuming retraining exercises on the part of employers; these would be essential for British employers in order to upgrade their workforces to Continental standards of competence. But an additional deterrent faced by employers is that not only would substantial retraining of employed adults be needed to meet these standards, but employees would not expect to lose existing levels of pay during retraining. British employers appear to be trapped; they have relied upon low skilled, limited choice, high output markets for which serious competition is emerging throughout the globe. Therefore, diversification and sophistication of product is necessary to overcome challenges presented by the low-cost mass-production capability of Pacific Rim and Southern and Eastern European countries, but taking this direction demands highly skilled and flexible workforces and trained supervisors:

> From the three sectors of manufacturing we have so far studied, it seems clear that the greater part of the British workforce is insufficiently skilled, flexible and polyvalent to be capable of meeting these challenges.
>
> (Steedman and Wagner 1989)

Under existing conditions and with little overt external pressure exerted upon them, it seems difficult to contemplate that employers would voluntarily make the long-term shifts in manpower policy needed to compensate for these deficiencies.

CONCLUDING COMMENTS

A number of key studies conducted in the early and middle years of the 1980s trace out the progress of employer training during this period. Initial studies indicated a lack of strategic intent in employer training efforts, which when converted into practice, were largely confined to training for short-term immediate job requirements or for remedial attention in the case of managers. The absence of a strategic element was compounded by the distance of senior management from training and developmental activities and their own lack of recognition of positive links between education, qualifications and managerial performance.

The mid-decade position, then, presented a generally lowly status for training activities, typified by a non-systematic approach to training. Government exhortations that training should be treated by employers as an 'investment' in human resources, involving long-term productivity gains secured through commitment to training, were defeated by a combination of the short-termism of company training ambitions, the lack of cost and benefit analyses of training undertaken by companies, and the perfunctory involvement by senior management representatives in training affairs. It appeared that training was receiving the traditional neglect offered to other aspects of personnel and industrial relations activity, a point which is discussed further in the following chapter.

Training in Britain showed that whilst expenditure on training had apparently increased by 1986–7, the underlying tendencies of companies to adopt 'knee-jerk' responses to the pressures surrounding them were maintained. Nevertheless, in the last years of the decade these pressures intensified: continuing warnings of the manifold implications to companies of the impending Single European Market were issued by the government, and the extent of the demographic changes to be faced by employers constantly reaffirmed through the media and government informational services. Technological advances with associated shifts in occupation and industry were also accelerating. Finally, at the end of the decade, revolutionary political, economic and social change swept across Eastern Europe, resulting in further sources of competition for domestic producers.

Against this background, a survey was undertaken by the author in 1989 to explore developments in employer philosophy and practice with regard to training. A full ten years of market-led regulation would provide an opportunity to examine the extent to which employers had accepted their 'prime responsibility' to invest in 'a strategy of training through life'. After all, if following ten years of market-led manpower policy, operating in the shadow of some of the broadest and widest-ranging economic and social changes this century had witnessed, a distinct shift in employer approach was not visible, considerable doubt would be cast on the value of the market-led approach in regulating manpower activity.

Chapter 6

Training and the personnel function

> 'It has fallen off a bit' – Personnel manager in the chemical industry, discussing training.
>
> (MacKay and Torrington 1986: 61)

BACKGROUND

Government aspirations to inculcate in employers 'a strategy of training through life' were scrutinised in the preceding chapter, where it was also pointed out that whilst welcoming any assistance to support training efforts, individual employers are unlikely to attach much weight to exhortations to expand their own training programmes unless observable and substantial benefits could be anticipated. Nevertheless, with rapid change taking place within the economy, organisations are being prompted by external pressures to examine the approaches they adopt for managing their operations, and in particular, for managing employees. In this sense, government encouragement for employers to strengthen their training efforts in the face of these pressures is at least timely.

It was with these thoughts in mind that a study on training and personnel practice in the private sector was undertaken in Scotland in 1989 with the aim of identifying the nature and extent of training provision and the factors which influence these.

THE SCOTTISH SURVEY

Questionnaires were distributed to 500 companies in the summer of 1989. The sample was stratified according to the divisions contained in the 1981 Standard Industrial Classification but distribution within each classification was made on a random basis. One hundred and six useable responses were returned, representing a response rate of 21 per cent. The response rate was undoubtedly influenced by the length and detail of the questionnaire (21 pages), and though rather modest, is well compensated by the wealth of material obtained. The majority of responses were received from companies operating in the service sector, with nearly a quarter of replies from respondents in distributing, retail and wholesale and 18 per cent of replies from financial services companies. However, 29 per cent of replies were received from a diverse range of manufacturing companies.

The size of company varied considerably. Categorisation according to number of employees provided three approximately equally-proportioned divisions comprised of small enterprises employing less than 50 people, medium employing between 50 and 500, and large companies with more than 500 employees. The classification is shown in Table 6.1.

As organisation size is considered to be an important factor in shaping personnel practice and training provision (Daniel and Millward 1983; MacKay and Torrington 1986: 49; Training Agency 1989), our analysis makes regular reference to these three categories and develops the small firm data for a more detailed examination of training in this sector in Chapter 7.

Though conducted in Scotland, the survey was not confined simply to Scottish-based companies. More than half of company or group head offices were located in Scotland, with one-fifth situated in England, and a minority in Europe and the USA. In total, the 106 companies employed some 82,095 people in Scotland, but more than half a million in the UK as a whole. Nevertheless, over half of the companies, including the majority of small concerns, located all their employees in Scotland.

Table 6.1: Company size by employee number

Size of company (number of employees)	Number of companies	% of companies
Less than 50 (Small)	37	35
50–500 (Medium)	37	35
Over 500 (Large)	30	28
No Reply	2	2

$(N = 106)$

The market and employment situation of the companies

Replies from the majority of companies indicated that they had experienced a buoyant year over the previous 12 months; increases in sales turnover were confirmed by 84 per cent of respondents, two-thirds expanded their product range and three-quarters increased the numbers of customers. Two-thirds of companies reported an increase in profits during the same period. If training provision is sensitive to external market conditions, it would appear that the underlying conditions for its maintenance or expansion were not unduly unfavourable.

Turning to employment conditions over the previous year, staffing levels generally had remained constant, but more than one-third of respondents replied that staffing of technical and professional posts had increased during the same period. Possibly reflecting the generally favourable market conditions, any tendency for change in staffing levels was two to three times more likely to be in the direction of growth rather than contraction, especially in medium and large companies. Three-quarters of companies replied that they intended to increase the use of new technology over the next 12 months, and among these, 18 per cent replied that they had 'concrete plans' to recruit specialised staff; 86 per cent would retrain existing employees in the use of new technology, indicating a dual approach by some companies.

Company plans for expansion might be compromised by unavailability of labour, however, for as Table 6.2 shows, a sizeable proportion of employers experienced difficulty in recruiting the professional, technical, managerial and skilled staff most in demand over the previous year.

The companies then appear to be operating in positive market conditions and many had expansion plans for the future. However, these ambitions could be frustrated by shortages of staff. When asked to detail factors contributing most to recruitment problems, over half (55 per cent) pointed to shortages of available skills, with the next most common reason given as 'uncompetitive pay levels', though this was offered in only 18 per cent of responses to the question.

The contextual conditions of buoyant market conditions threatened by predominantly skills shortage based recruitment problems point to two related factors, namely, headaches for personnel specialists unable to recruit staff to sustain organisational growth and in consequence, a potentially favourable background for companies to undertake training for existing employees. As maintaining staff levels appropriate for organisational needs is primarily a functional responsibility for the

Table 6.2: Degree of difficulty in recruiting employees

Occupational group	% of companies reporting high difficulty in recruiting
Skilled	38
Technical and Professional	28
Managerial	26
Clerical and Administrative	6

$(N = 91)$

personnel specialist (Sisson 1989: 3) we first examine the role of personnel management in organisations and in particular its suitability and readiness to discharge training responsibilities.

PERSONNEL MANAGEMENT UNDER PRESSURE

Under pressure from diverse directions it comes as no surprise that in recent years a great deal of management thinking has attempted to get to grips with the concept of 'strategy' and its relevance to the management of people (Fox 1974; Purcell and Sisson 1983). In essence, the term strategy refers to the relationship between planning and securing the organisation's long-term goals (Marginson *et al.* 1988: 184). The extent to which British companies have adopted planned strategies in this sense is highly questionable, tending instead toward a short-term perspective in seeking their profit objectives; this is demonstrated in particular by the priority given by companies to offering generous dividend payments to stockholders in order to satisfy institutional investor interests and to ward off threats from predatory take-overs: 'For (big market investors) a dividend cut is the ultimate sign of management weakness and ineptitude. Dividend policy is considered crucial to a company's share price' (*Guardian*, 22 September 1990).

In short, these companies are responding rationally to the market conditions within which they operate, which represents a central feature of government policy. A 1990 survey showed that dividend payments grew by an average of 19.2 per cent over the previous two years, far in excess of prevailing inflation rates and during a period when capital investment has been consistently low by international standards (*Financial Times*, 20 February 1991). Figures taken from the Business Statistics Office and *Bank of England Quarterly Bulletin* demonstrate similar inflated dividend trends, explained as a 'defensive measure during a period when takeover activity was at an all-time high' (*Labour Research*, September 1990: 9–10). Unfortunately such 'measures' serve to sustain the dynamics of 'short-termism' into which the domestic economy is locked, and by subordinating investment and development to the imperatives of divided distribution, cast serious doubt upon the extent to which companies operating to these criteria are able to adopt a planned, more strategic view of their operations.

With physical investment constrained through short-term obligations, it is perhaps not surprising that employee relations matters have tended to be peripheral to and excluded from strategic or high-level decision taking; the very nature of the contractual employment relationship is short-term and in consequence, 'bottom line' calculations can tempt employers to treat employees merely as 'necessary evils' to be channelled through discipline and manipulation into undertaking managerially defined and controlled activities. Employment relations would involve specialist practitioners (personnel managers) patrolling the areas bounded by management discretion, legal protections for employees and assertions of the market strengths of the employees themselves, especially when represented collectively through trade unions. Arguably, one of the responsibilities of personnel managers would be to act as a filter or barrier between management decision-makers and the employee recipients of their decisions, though one outcome of this would be equivalent exile for personnel managers, who, pushed to the margins of corporate activity, would be offered little scope to get on board the decision-making or strategic flagship.

Moreover, it might be thought that little advantage would be gained by including personnel within the ranks of senior management: corporate decisions involve the hard issues of finance and of production, of marketing and of maintaining corporate growth through acquisition (or avoiding it through satisfying investors); all activities controlled and directed unilaterally by management with no requirement or internal pressure for employee inputs.[1] In the smaller concern, proximity between owner-manager and staff obviated the need for bureaucratic personnel procedures (see Rainnie 1989) or specialised staff to introduce, implement and operate such procedures.

Faced with these restrictions, a recurrent theme for personnel has been to find a secure and honourable position among its management peers, a quest not helped by the occupation's original and continuing concern with the welfare of employees (Niven 1967), its range of loosely connected and unrelated activities (the so-called 'trash can' approach), its weak professional image (Daniel and Millward 1983) and its apparent failure to bring lasting peace to industrial relations. All in all, there have been few periods during its existence when personnel has not been suffering from a mighty personality problem. In the last few years, however, hopes for practitioners may have risen for, as indicated above, across both public and private sectors, widespread contextual changes have been occurring which serve to shift the activities and priorities of organisations. These shocks have had the effect of putting personnel activities under sharper focus, whilst potentially offering personnel specialists the chance of some upward mobility in management eyes.

The main developments can be summarised as follows: pressures of competition have increased, both in the commercial sector and public service sectors. In the former, for example, Japan has been joined by other Pacific Rim countries in producing quality goods cheaply and effectively. Competition from both Western and now Eastern Europe has grown as commercial and political barriers have been removed.

In the public domain, competitive markets have been thrust on to industries and organisations through privatisation and compulsory competitive tendering accompanied by the vast sweep of labour market reforms enacted over the past ten years. Moreover, in both public and private sectors, competition has not been asserted solely through price; product quality, reliability expressed through longer and more generous periods of warranty, extending the range of products and services, punctual delivery and standards of after-sales service have become the foundation stones upon which competition is expressed, all summarised in the ubiquitous though meaningless sloganising of management to pursue standards of corporate 'excellence' on behalf of clients. The drive for quality has been proclaimed through management eagerness to achieve 'total quality management' (*Times Higher Education Supplement*, 6 April 1990), zero defects and the like (Wickens 1987: 61–74). This competitive tightening has been given additional force by technological evolutions which allow for continually improving standards of production and service to customers.

As we saw from the recruitment difficulties faced by survey respondents, these developments are occurring at a time when skill shortages are becoming ever more apparent. Demographic and educational trends are combining to reduce numbers of young people available for work immediately following their post-compulsory education, a position exacerbated by the legacy of the traditional failure to train, leaving shortages of skills required to operate, service and (crucially) manage the advances in technology at standards necessary to meet the new competitive pressures.

Hence, the government's call for continuing lifetime development of employees has been made at a time when organisations are operating within an economic environment which places considerable demands upon the quality, adaptability and commitment of employees. If the demand for labour is, as economists say, derived from the nature of the product which labour is called upon to produce, and if quality and reliability of product are inseparable from the processes of production, then it follows that labour itself must meet the standards necessary to compete on these terms. Muted and uncommitted employee compliance to contractionally sanctioned management orders will not be sufficient to meet these demands.

One manifestation of this requirement for committed and adaptable staff has been the move away (at least in the titles of practitioners and their departments) from 'personnel management' toward 'human resource management'. Human resource management (HRM) aims to treat employees as organisational assets in whom it is required to invest to gain the skills needed in order to thrive in the contemporary competitive climate. Moreover, in a shrinking pool of labour, companies cannot afford to lose the value of investments made in their key employees, either through leaving or by reduced motivation in disgruntled workers. HRM has therefore been associated principally with changing the work performance of employees, including managers, in order to fulfil organisational priorities, by adopting a range of integrated policies (representing the current organisational emphasis on 'culture') designed to enhance staff performance and to retain and massage their commitment.

Protagonists claim that HRM has resulted in an approach to staff management typified by paying close attention to individual performance, its stimulation, monitoring, assessment and rewards, to expanding the range of tasks and responsibilities undertaken by both individuals and groups and by treating employee performance as an integral part of corporate performance, shifting personnel activities more closely into line with managerial requirements, and importantly, personnel activities into a key managerial concern. HRM, to personnel, could open the door for wider recognition and advancement long sought by its practitioners.

If organisations are indeed shifting voluntarily toward this HRM type of people-centred approach, then it is feasible that government plans to raise levels of worker performance though life-time programmes of learning and training at work are being adopted by UK organisations: the policy of creating a competitive market for both product and labour would then appear to be an effective one in raising skill levels. One of the central tenets of the HRM approach is that 'the HRM model tends to focus on skill development' (Thurley 1990). The diagrammatic representation of HRM presented by Storey (1989: 7) would seem to confirm its centrality in enhancing the performance and motivation of staff. If, on the other hand, the position with regard to training is as limited in ambition and expenditure as earlier studies have suggested, it is difficult to see how organisations are genuinely following and implementing a policy of HRM based on skill development.

THE RESPONSIBILITY OF PERSONNEL FOR TRAINING

It will be recalled from the previous chapter that a central problem for training was the complacency of senior management towards its provision. It might be anticipated that personnel specialists would adopt a more constructive approach toward training provision, especially as the literature makes clear that training and its attendant activities comprise '*the* vital component' of human resource management (Storey 1989: 14–15, original emphasis). Pratt and Bennett emphasise that notwithstanding areas of ambiguity surrounding some aspects of the personnel specialist role there is no confusion surrounding its responsibility for training: 'The Personnel and Training Department will be responsible for the development and review of training plans, programmes and preparation of training budgets' (1985: 8). Livy also posits that not only is 'training . . . normally regarded as a specialist function of personnel management' (1988: 140), but that it is in the *forefront* of personnel management (1988: 139). In their survey of 350 personnel practitioners, MacKay and Torrington (1986) examine links between personnel and training practice. It is worth considering their findings in some depth as they help to reveal how personnel's lack of confidence has helped to condemn training to secondary positions in managerial thinking and practice.

The dominant formal role of training indicated by the above commentators is confirmed by their study: 83 per cent of respondents undertake training, and for one in ten, it takes up a substantial proportion of personnel time. According to the authors: 'Training in one form or another takes up a similar amount of time in our respondents' jobs as recruitment/selection and employee relations' (1986: 48). Not only did training take up considerable time, but practitioners claimed that they enjoy a considerable degree of discretion in its exercise, and that, after manpower planning, the activity had been the one that had most increased in importance over the previous three years. Over 10 per cent of respondents identified training 'as being the central activity of the personnel function' (1986: 48).

But findings from the survey show that the formal centrality of training is not matched by its practice. Over a quarter of respondents pointed to a decline in the time and effort afforded to training over the past three years (1986: 59), a time when publicity and controversy surrounding training practice in Britain was at peak levels following publication of a number of condemnatory reports (see Chapter 5). Subsequent interviews conducted among a fifth of the respondents demonstrated that training provision was indeed strongly related to outside pressures; only a minority of personnel specialists saw training in positive terms:

> Only a few interviewees suggested that training was a good thing to do in itself. Indeed many respondents seemed to have a somewhat lack-lustre attitude towards training. Training was the single most often mentioned aspect of personnel work that was least liked.
>
> (1986: 61)

Two main explanations can be offered for the offhand approach adopted by personnel to one of its main responsibilities; first, that training, with its long-term perspectives and lack of immediate or visual organisational impact does not enjoy support among managerial colleagues. Second, the personnel manager, wishing to escape from a traditional identification with employees and their welfare toward a closer managerial orientation, 'increasingly espouses the same set of values as his colleagues' (1986: 62). These, as we saw earlier, tend not to include training. Indeed, much of the blame for the poor showing of training is attributed to personnel's managerial peers, seeking 'a clear short-term pay-off, cut it out or put if off' approach reinforced by disinterest among personnel itself to 'the long-term investment and thoroughness that characterizes effective training' (MacKay and Torrington 1986: 63).

Since the survey was conducted in 1984, there have been signs of growing awareness among personnel of its responsibilities toward training. In predicting the major issues to be faced by personnel in the present decade, Chapman pointed to training and development as towering above all other matters as the area of most concern (1990: 32). Whether practitioners can or want to take up this challenge is another question, but in the absence of imposed regulatory mechanisms, it is likely that only personnel and training managers could have sufficient specialised familiarity with the value and techniques of training to be able to promote its claims effectively to senior management. As the MacKay and Torrington survey demonstrates, personnel has considerable discretion with respect to the practice of both training and management development (1986: 48): what it seems to lack is either the confidence or willingness to take advantage of these favourable conditions.

This takes us back to the point that personnel has tended to occupy a subordinate place within the managerial hierarchy of many organisations. Arguably, the function would be able to pursue a training emphasis more persuasively from a platform of equality with managerial colleagues. The present survey set out to establish the structural potential of personnel to pursue a more active and combative approach toward training provision.

A number of commentators have suggested that as a consequence of the many changes noted earlier, the potential of personnel to contribute to organisational priorities has received a boost. It seems likely that if personnel is gaining a more substantial managerial presence, then this should at least be reflected in its formal status within management circles, as demonstrated by membership on the Board of Directors. Earlier national studies by Daniel and Millward (1983) and Millward and Stevens (1986) established that during the early years of the decade, about 42–43 per cent of companies had specialist representation of personnel on their Board of Directors. This figure, however, jumped to 70 per cent representation in organisations with 10,000 or more employees (1986: 36). The present survey asked the more restrictive question as to whether there was a Personnel Director on the Board of Directors, and the proportion was considerably lower at 22 per cent. If personnel is present at Board level, in only a minority of companies would it appear that it is identified exclusively in personnel terms.

Our findings that Board representation for personnel was reported by only a minority of companies can be contrasted with findings from another contemporary study in which over 60 per cent of 'heads of personnel' were found to have a place on the main Board of Directors, where representation would potentially offer greater scope for strategic level involvement (Price Waterhouse 1990). Almost certainly, these differences in representation can be traced primarily to the size dispersion of the two studies. Small companies were not included in the Price Waterhouse project, and in common with other studies, our survey showed much higher levels of Board representation in larger concerns; 52 per cent of enterprises with more than 500 employees replied that they had a personnel director.

A further sign of elevation for personnel might be found in the range of personnel activities said to be undertaken in the enterprise. To try and reduce the manifold problems of disentangling policy from practice (see Brewster *et al.* 1981; Marginson and Sisson 1988: 120) we asked respondents to detail whether a range of personnel policies, associated with contemporary HRM practice, were actually in operation (or were intended for operation) in their companies. Findings are shown in Table 6.3.

As might be expected, these policies were more commonly reported by larger organisations. Applying policies for performance appraisal, recognition of equal opportunities, performance-related pay, briefing groups and the like does point to companies taking some action to secure employee loyalty and commitment. With regard to loyalty, at least, they may be enjoying some success. Whilst difficulties in recruitment were widespread, respondents reported far fewer problems with staff retention: 13 per cent of respondents experienced high levels of difficulty in retaining skilled manual occupations, but only 7 per cent reported similar problems for their managers and 5 per cent for technical and professional staff. It may well be that attempts by companies to offer more sophisticated and rewarding personnel approaches to their employees is helping to account for the apparently low turnover of staff.

Whether numbers of personnel directors and the findings on personnel practice reported above reflect genuine upward advancement for personnel is hard to say. We do know that through the recession of the early 1980s, the numbers and institutional status of personnel remained fairly stable (Millward and Stevens 1986: 41). With widespread changes in economic and labour market circumstances, it seems likely that personnel would, at the very least retain its position, or, more likely, make some advance. Certainly, the Price Waterhouse researchers were able to report that 'half of those responsible for personnel are involved in the development of corporate strategy from the outset. A further three out of ten are consulted during its formulation' (1990: 12). In larger companies at least, it appears that personnel can occupy a managerial platform from which the promotion of training could be launched if they have the self-belief and the desire to do so.

THE STATUS OF TRAINING

We have seen that, formally training comprises an important part of the responsibilities of the personnel function and for this reason, training activities are linked functionally to personnel in most organisations

Table 6.3: Personnel policies in operation

Personnel policy	Currently in operation (%)	Intending to introduce	Not in practice and not intended
Job Evaluation	58	17	26
Performance Appraisal	78	9	13
Performance-Related Pay	50	14	36
Employee Share Scheme	29	8	63
Single Status (Harmonisation)	14	10	74
Quality Circles	17	16	66
Equal Opportunity Policy	78	7	16
Briefing Groups	48	10	41
JCCs	34	10	55
Joint H & S Committee	48	11	40

(N = 94)

(Kenney and Reid 1988: 36; MacKay and Torrington 1986: 48). In practice, however, we need to ask how well-established is this link and how well-functioning the mechanisms are for its operation. This question takes on more significance in the light of MacKay and Torrington's findings that training is one of personnel's least favoured activities.

Examining these structural linkages, it rapidly became evident that there are major differences in training responsibilities between large and smaller organisations. For this reason, findings are presented according to organisational size.

Small companies (*N* = 37)

Very few small companies (maximum fifty employees) have a specialist training function. Decisions on training and its expenditure are made by the Board or by senior management. A company director took the position of the most senior trainer in 52 per cent of cases, followed by 'other senior manager' in 12 per cent of small companies. The specialist knowledge of the trainer seems extremely limited, with two-thirds having no formal training or associated qualifications (e.g. personnel studies) whatsoever, and only 7 per cent claiming either IPM or ITD membership or possessing a relevant degree.

In more than half of cases (57 per cent) the senior trainer reports to the managing director, and in a quarter, directly to the Board. Four out of five small company trainers spend less than 10 per cent of their time on training activities, and in nearly a third of companies there was no designated department responsible for co-ordinating training and no established staff allocated to training. Thirty-seven per cent of companies indicated the Board as having direct responsibility for co-ordinating training and 85 per cent pointed to Board or senior management responsibility for allocating training expenditure. Personnel presence and involvement was rarely found across any of these areas.

Medium companies ($N = 37$)

In these companies, we see growing personnel inputs, though again, with a high proportion of non-specialist involvement in training. Thirty-one per cent of respondents pointed to a company director as the most senior trainer, followed by 23 per cent who indicated a plant/branch manager. Seventeen per cent nominated a personnel director as the most senior trainer. Even in these companies, however, over half the senior trainers had no relevant qualifications, though nearly a quarter did have some combination of IPM, ITD or degree relevant to personnel affairs. Again, some 80 per cent of senior trainers were reported to spend less than 10 per cent of their time on training, though 3 per cent spent more than half of their time on this activity.

In two-thirds of cases, the senior trainer reported directly to the managing director (none reported directly to a personnel director or manager, though in 17 per cent of cases, of course, the personnel director had previously been indicated as the senior trainer and would not be expected to report in that direction). As with small companies, a high proportion (94 per cent) of respondents said that training expenditure was determined at Board or senior management levels. In medium companies, 19 per cent of respondents reported that no specific department took overall responsibility for training, with 22 per cent pointing to the personnel department. One in five respondents said that numbers of training staff had increased over the past 12 months.

Large companies (N = 30)

In these companies, we see rather more involvement by personnel interests in training. The most senior trainer in 43 per cent of cases was the training manager, and in 29 per cent, the personnel director. One quarter of senior trainers had no relevant qualifications but almost one half (46 per cent) did have these qualifications. The senior trainer was most likely to be directly responsible to either a personnel director or manager (43 per cent) or to a general manager (36 per cent) but not to the managing director (4 per cent) or Board (7 per cent). Training expenditure decisions would be made either at Board level (44 per cent) or by senior management (37 per cent) and in only 7 per cent of cases by personnel.

Departmental responsibility for training lay either with personnel (53 per cent) or training (33 per cent). In only 16 per cent of cases did senior trainers spend less than 10 per cent of their time on training, and 56 per cent spent more than half their time on training matters. Fifty-five per cent of large companies had increased their training staffing over the previous year.

SUMMARY

We have seen that there are very good commercial reasons for companies to take training seriously. For this to happen there needs to be appropriate representational structures within companies capable of promoting, co-ordinating and evaluating training. Though training is acknowledged as primarily a responsibility of personnel, recent research indicates that in practice, personnel tends to neglect this responsibility.

Though based on relatively small numbers, our studies show that in aggregate neither training nor personnel is organisationally in a strong position to pursue training activities. Small companies rarely use a specialist training function and responsibility for training is undertaken usually by a director or senior manager, for whom training typically represents only a minor part of overall activities. In these companies, large numbers of designated trainers lack any formal training credentials. Designated senior trainers in medium companies, employing up to 500 employees, were also largely unqualified and in the majority of cases spend only a small proportion of time on training activities.

It is only when we come to larger organisations that we see a change in these patterns with the emergence of a professionalised personnel and training function. Even here, though, a quarter of senior trainers were unadorned by formal qualification. Training expenditure decisions were usually made at Board or senior management level and rarely by personnel alone, raising the question as to how much discretion personnel/ training enjoys in raising and stabilising training expenditure. According to the Mackay and Torrington findings, personnel managers themselves consider that they have considerable discretion in this exercise, though our findings suggest that in the majority of cases and especially in smaller companies it would be difficult to find the expertise upon which to build such discretion, where it exists. Even in larger companies, in only a handful of cases did personnel enjoy the independence to make training expenditure decisions, though, of course, in many of these companies there would be personnel directors available to pursue a case for training at Board level, if they were inclined to do so. The evidence suggests, of course, that this is unlikely.

Having noted the rather weak organisational position occupied typically by training interests, we can now turn to the nature of training activities pursued by the survey companies.

Chapter 7

Training in practice

> Ten years ago, management was preoccupied with survival. Today, the concern is with the future. In such circumstances, there is a realistic prospect that more employers will regard skills training as an important investment essential to future competitiveness, not simply as a current cost to be minimised.
>
> (CBI 1989: 29)

INTRODUCTION

In the previous chapter, we saw that training expenditure is typically determined at senior levels within the organisation, both in small and larger concerns. This finding is perhaps surprising, as many commentators assume that training decisions are taken 'at a low level of the business' and 'it is rare for the Board to be involved' (TUC 1989: 11). In confronting this assumption, our findings would suggest that two potential outcomes for the elevated locus of training expenditure decisions present themselves; it could offer valuable support to training provision, or alternatively, indicate that training determination might be a volatile process, fluctuating in accordance with senior management priorities or even pushed to the margins of their main areas of activity. The levels of expertise and time offered to training activity by senior trainers does rather point toward the latter possibility and thereby help to sustain the belief that training provision is typically determined at a low level within management.

The present chapter analyses in greater depth the amount of training expenditure undertaken by companies and, in particular, identifies areas where training expenditure is concentrated and the ways in which it is allocated. We examine the extent to which training is being treated as an integral part of personnel policy and identify instances of where training feeds into a more investment-orientated role for the treatment of staff. In this respect, the following areas are traced in closer detail: usage made by employers of government-backed training programmes; management and technology training; and the degrees to which employees are involved in determining the directions and extent of training.

TRAINING EXPENDITURE

The CBI statement quoted above illustrates one consistent failing identified by virtually every published report on expenditure on training in Britain; that domestic companies perceive and treat training expenditure as a cost rather than longer-term investment. Despite the CBI's optimism, the extent to which there is indeed a 'realistic prospect' that companies will think more in investment terms with regard to their employees has yet to be established. But as we have seen from earlier studies, inclinations toward 'short-term costism' have been bolstered by the order of priorities established by the organisation and further reinforced by a meek acceptance (or even preference; see MacKay and Torrington 1986: 63) by personnel of these priorities. Further, we can see that the context for employers to adopt a longer-term view of their scarce 'human resources' conflicts with the dynamics of an unregulated free market which mitigates against long-term employee development. The CBI quote actually recognises these market realities; when pressures are tight and companies are fighting for survival, then long-term planning associated with training is difficult to maintain. Hence, in the absence of other cultural or legal controls, employers will only train 'for life' when reasonably assured that they want to keep the same employees 'for life'.

A pertinent and related sign of the institutional weakness and dependence of training on factors outside its control has been the absence of an identifiable training budget. Without a measure of independence of action, it is scarcely surprising that training expenditure has tended to fluctuate according to the short-term financial demands identified by senior management. It was with these thoughts in mind that we set out to determine the extent of these financial limitations today.

Almost half (45 per cent) of the respondents confirmed that they do have a budget in the form of an identifiable and specific financial allocation made annually. As might be expected, this practice was more widespread in large companies, nearly three-quarters of whom reported an allocated budget, contrasting with 18 per cent of small concerns. More than half (51 per cent) of companies reported no budget allocation made for training. The remainder (4 per cent) did not know whether there was a budget or not.

Even for those companies with a training budget, weaknesses are apparent. Two-thirds of these companies reported that budgeted training expenditure amounted to less than 2 per cent of total employment costs, a figure which contrasts sharply with reported figures for countries such as West Germany or France. An indication of persisting vulnerability of training to prevailing trading conditions was shown by 40 per cent of companies with budgets stating that these vary each year according to previous performance or profit levels. Assuming a direct relationship between performance criteria and training budget, poor performance, possibly exacerbated by skill shortages or non-optimal use of new technologically based opportunities, could be reinforced through further short-term cost reductions, rather than longer-term investment expansion in training expenditure.

On a more positive note, 58 per cent of respondents with a training budget reported that their budgets had increased over the past year, but bearing in mind the favourable trading conditions experienced by the majority of companies, and the dependent links with performance reported by the above 40 per cent of companies, this finding is not too surprising. Among the whole sample, just over half (53 per cent) replied that training expenditure had increased, including 85 per cent of large companies. Of some concern would be the 22 per cent of respondents who were unable to state whether their training expenditures had changed at all over the past 12 months. Looking forward to the next 12 months, 52 per cent considered that training expenditure would increase, and a third of respondents anticipated an unchanged expenditure.

The survey also requested a quantification of annual expenditure on direct training activities. By specifying *direct* expenditure, we hoped to simplify any calculating procedures for respondents and consequently, we assume that wage costs have not been included in the figures given. In retrospect, however, it might have been preferable to ask respondents to specify additional labour costs incurred in the training process. As might be expected, many companies were unable or unwilling to provide figures, but sixty, representing 57 per cent of the sample, did offer this information, which is itemised in Table 7.1.

The amounts spent on training are appreciably smaller than those found in *Training in Britain* which provided an inclusive figure of £809 training expenditure per employee at 1986/7 prices (Training Agency 1989: 21). Part of the reasons for the differences between the figures can be explained by the different methods of calculation used, with the

Table 7.1: Mean training expenditures

Size of organisation	Number	Mean annual expenditure per employee* (£)
Small	21	73
Medium	21	87
Large	18	111

Including part-time employees.

present survey using those figures offered by the companies themselves for their training *expenditure* and *budgets*, whilst the larger survey drew its conclusions for total training *costs* calculated from a range of data provided by the companies. Whilst there may be differences between stated expenditures and aggregate costs, it is, nevertheless, difficult to reconcile the substantial differences between these figures.

As expected, on average, smaller companies tend to spend less per employee than middle range and larger enterprises. Even so, considerable variations within the size of groupings were apparent; the lowest spending small company, a distributor of petroleum products, claimed not to have spent anything at all on its twenty-three employees, whilst the highest per capita spender, a technological consultancy with eleven employees, spent nearly £500 per employee over the past 12 months. The lowest spending medium company, in the hospitality industry, spent £10 per employee for its 240 staff, whilst the highest spender, a high technology company with fifty-five employees, spent over £1,800 per employee. Large companies displayed similar variations in their patterns of expenditure; the lowest spender, located in the service and repairs sector, offered £9,000 for its 1,500 employees, an average of £6 an employee per annum, and the highest, an oil industry company, an average of £1,500 annually for each of its 5,000 employees. Training expenditure was also disaggregated on an industry sector basis (Table 7.2).

Sector disaggregation suggests a degree of polarisation between those companies whose training expenditures are low or very low, 59 per cent of responding companies, and those with designated 'high' or 'very high' expenditure (30 per cent), with few companies in the median ranges of expenditure. A concentration of very low expenditure was found in the distribution/leisure services industries.

Table 7.2: Training expenditure by SIC*

Standard Industrial Classification (SIC)	Expenditure				
	Very low	Low	Medium	High	Very high
Energy and Water Supply	–	–	–	–	1
Manufacture of Metals, Mineral Products, Chemicals	1	–	–	–	1
Metal Goods, Engineering and Vehicle Manufacturing	1	2	–	1	2
Other Manufacturing	8	3	–	–	2
Construction	3	–	1	1	–
Distribution, Wholesale, Retail, Hotel and Catering	7	2	–	2	2
Transport and Communication	2	3	2	–	–
Banking, Insurance and Financial Services	2	–	–	1	2
Other Services	1	–	3	–	3
	25 (42%)	10 (17%)	7 (12%)	5 (8%)	13 (22%)

* Average training expenditure per employee.

Key:
Very low expenditure   = £0–£50 average expenditure per employee per annum.
Low expenditure   = £51–£100 average expenditure per employee per annum.
Medium expenditure   = £101–£150 average expenditure per employee per annum.
High expenditure   = £151–£200 average expenditure per employee per annum.
Very high expenditure   = £201+ average expenditure per employee per annum.

The overall figures confirm that whilst the actual and proposed increases in training expenditure provided by respondents give grounds for cautious optimism, it appears that the funding base from which these increases derive is extremely low in the majority of instances and in only a few cases could represent a significant input into human resource investment. This leads to further difficulty for training specialists, for the disparity between figures obtained in this survey and those given in the wider *Training in Britain* study indicates some of the problems which may be faced by personnel and training managers in trying to quantify and justify expenditure on human resources to sceptical senior managers and their financial advisors.

Bearing in mind the significant differences between the Scottish study figures and the statistics presented in the *Training in Britain* study, one question that needs to be addressed is the extent to which these figures provide an accurate representation of company training expenditure. Fortunately, other figures have recently been disclosed which help to establish that *actual* annual expenditures on training rarely exceed £200 for every employee.

A briefing paper prepared by the Labour Party employment spokesperson has used data extracted from the 1988 Labour Cost Survey to indicate employer training costs for five main industrial sectors. Mean expenditures are detailed in Table 7.3 along with the equivalent sums obtained from the present research.

With training and development taking a generally lowly place in the affairs of management, it might be unwise to assume that companies have maintained precise records of their actual or budgeted expenditure. We would not expect this to be the case and recognise that we are not dealing with absolutes when comparing these figures. Indeed, if training were highly integrated into the human resource practices of companies, as appears to be the case in many large Japanese companies (see Chapter 4), it may be impractical to extract training expenditures. In Britain, however, it is unlikely that such 'constraints' apply to the majority of companies: the status of training as an occupation and the amount of management time attached to it by those primarily responsible for its provision suggests that such integration has yet to occur within domestic management practice. For the moment, at least, training remains a peripheral activity, and as confirmed by the studies reported above, an activity generally dominated by low expenditure, even when compared with the provision of employee benefits:

> What is disturbing is that across the five sectors surveyed, when labour costs are aggregated many employers are spending more on 'Benefits in Kind' – luncheon vouchers, other meal vouchers and net cost to employers for goods provided free or below cost from employers – assistance with housing and other services such as company cars, health, recreation, canteens, removal expenses, etc, than they are on training . . . . When these figures are disaggregated across industry . . . , it is clear that some employers spend more on luncheon vouchers than they do on training.
>
> (McLeish 1990: 8)

INVOLVEMENT IN GOVERNMENT TRAINING SCHEMES

In Chapter 3 we indicated the importance attached by the State to training schemes for young and unemployed people as part of the

Table 7.3: Average training costs in 1988* and 1989** compared

Sector	1989			1988 Labour Cost Survey
	No. of companies	Expenditure/ employee (£)		Expenditure/ employee (£)
Energy and Water	1	1500		118
Manufacture of Metals, Mineral & Chemicals	2	223		
Metal Goods, Engineering, Vehicle	6	297	Manufacturing	64
Other Manufacturing	14	59		
Construction	4	40		46
Distribution, Wholesale, Recreation, Hotel & Catering	15	142	Distribution	32
Transport and Communications	5	81		
Bank, Insurance Financial Services	8	187	Banking	159
Other Services	5	158		

(N = 60)

* Excludes wage costs.
** Refers to direct expenditure.

Source: 1988 Labour Cost Survey, reproduced in McLeish 1990: table 2.

approach to align labour market supply with the demands of a changing economy. The two major programmes which dominated the latter part of the 1980s, and which were still actively in operation when the survey was conducted, were the Youth Training Scheme (YTS) for 16–18-year-olds and Employment Training (ET) for older unemployed, both or which had been promoted as a major part of the restructuring of the labour market.

Through the Department of Employment it was also emphasised that these schemes were intended to deliver high-quality training designed to raise overall skill levels and simultaneously fulfil employers' staffing needs. For this reason, both schemes have been heavily dependent upon co-operation and participation by employers for their successful operation. We therefore set out to examine whether the two major schemes were being used by employers and, equally important, to investigate reasons for their use or non-use. In particular, we wished to determine the extent to which use of government schemes integrates with other personnel approaches adopted by companies and whether an identifiable strategic pattern encompassing government training schemes emerges.

Employer participation in the Youth Training Scheme

Just over half (55 per cent) of the employers claimed to participate in YTS, with participation more common in larger companies (67 per cent) than small (39 per cent). The most common reason for non-participation, given by one-third of non-participants, was the 'inappropriateness' of the scheme to respondent needs. A further quarter replied that they did not use YTS as they offered their own training schedules. One-third of non-participants said that they had previously participated but subsequently withdrew, but with small numbers of companies, no firm pattern of reasons for withdrawal emerged.

In order to ascertain the prime motives for company participation, respondents were asked to rank in order of priority their reasons for participating in the scheme. Table 7.4 lists the rank order of reasons.

A picture emerges which suggests a polarisation of use for YTS; employers either incline to YTS for instrumental recruitment purposes, or they respond to public concern to train young people as a demonstration of social concern for them. It is interesting that larger companies, especially, tended to participate in YTS for these apparently more altruistic reasons. Over one-third of large company respondents placed 'social concern' as their highest priority reason for participation, compared with a fifth of small firms and only one out of seventeen

Table 7.4: Priority ranking of company participation in YTS

Reason for participation	No. of first rankings	Mean ranking*
Cost-effective recruitment approach	16	2.8
Opportunity to train young people	14	2.4
Social concern for young people	9	3.1
Integrates with apprenticeship	8	3.5
Overcome specific company labour shortages	7	3.6
Overcome general company labour shortages	0	4.3
Provide skills for new technology	0	5.1
No reply	3	–

(*N* = 57)

* Mean score of all rankings achieved.

medium-size firm participants. Smaller companies, in particular, were more likely to be attracted to YTS as a 'cost-effective approach' to recruitment, with eight out of twelve small respondents giving this as their primary reason for participation, compared with 28 per cent of medium companies and 19 per cent of large. Small companies were also more likely than larger companies to retain trainees at the conclusion of their training period.

Respondents were also asked to indicate the occupational areas in which trainees were involved in their companies. Details are shown in Table 7.5.

It can be seen that the most common occupation for YTS provision was in clerical and administrative placement, used by more than half of participating employers (30 from 57). This could well account for the relatively low proportion of employers (6 per cent) reporting high recruitment difficulties for these occupations.

Despite reported shortages by respondents of skilled manual employees, only a relatively modest number of companies were applying the scheme for craft trades, and as the priority rankings given by respondents in Table 7.4 indicate, the use of YTS to 'overcome specific company labour shortages' was given low priority by employers and even lower was its use to overcome 'general shortages' faced by the company. By far the lowest priority to respondents, however, was the use of YTS to provide skills for new technology, one of the

Table 7.5: Occupational areas for YTS usage

YTS occupational area	% of firms using*
Clerical and Administration	53
Construction/Craft	27
Engineering/Production	27
Marketing/Sales/Retail	22
Finance/Accounts	15
'All Areas'	6
Computer/Electronics	2

$(N = 57)$

* Firms could use YTS in more than one occupation.

acknowledged areas of shortage for both survey respondents and in the country generally. It appears then that many employers either use YTS to recruit staff to essentially routine positions, especially for clerical and administrative tasks, or they respond to exhortations to offer training to young people, possibly through an expression of social concern for them.

Employer participation in Employment Training

If the responses of employers to the use of YTS raise doubts as to its utility in meeting skill shortages, we are left in little doubt with regard to employer orientations to Employment Training. A very substantial majority of companies (88 per cent) were not participating in the scheme, and of these, only three hinted that they had intentions to participate in the future. Of the twelve companies participating in the scheme one intended to withdraw, and three were uncertain as to their future intentions. Only two companies expect to increase the number of trainees, which should not be too difficult; the eleven companies who provided figures, employing in excess of 7,500 people in Scotland, reported a total between them of twenty-five ET trainees.

With such a small number of participants, it was unrealistic to identify any dominant trends for ET involvement. But for non-involvement, a pattern did emerge in that of sixty companies giving reasons for non-participation, eighteen (32 per cent) regarded the scheme as inappropriate for their needs, and fifteen (25 per cent) simply saw the scheme as not being required for their company. Only a very small fraction attributed their non-participation to objections by trade unions opposed to ET.

On the basis of the survey findings there seems to be little evidence that the major contemporary government-sponsored schemes, operating in a climate of accumulating skill and staff shortages, are making much impact in combatting these shortages or are finding their way into any strategic company training plans.

In the light of this failure, it is perhaps not surprising that alternative approaches to skill acquisition for young people are being explored by the government as YTS gives way to 'New Youth Training', to be developed and monitored through a new TEC system which aims to co-ordinate publicly sponsored schemes more closely with local employer needs. The most radical innovation is the use of training credits in pilot projects covering about 45,000 school leavers and currently underway in ten TECs and one LEC in Scotland. Training credits, varying in value from about £500 to £5,000, provide an entitlement for school leavers to receive training to approved standards (to a minimum Level 2 of the NCVQ scales). Under this scheme, young people, whether employed or not, will be able to acquire training appropriate to their needs as guided by locally signalled skill demands and through advice given by the Careers Service. It is hoped that the TECs will be able to monitor and direct both training standards and co-ordinate trainee with employer needs.

With regard to ET, it seems difficult to see how, in its present form, this programme is ever to find favour with employers, let alone attract potential trainees, who have signalled their considerable doubts about its capability to enhance their employment prospects through mass abstention and premature withdrawal from the scheme (Employment Committee 1990).

MANAGEMENT TRAINING AND DEVELOPMENT

The poor educational background of most British managers and the dismal failure of their employers to provide them with training and opportunities for development has been well documented (Handy *et al.* 1988; Constable and McCormick 1987; Mangham and Silver 1986). Whilst initiatives to expand educational provision are underway (see Chapter 5), time will be necessary for the effects to filter through into managerial circles. On the other hand, one might expect that employers would be able to seize an early initiative with regard to their own training and developmental priorities.

A major step recommended by Handy and Constable and McCormick was the expansion of professional management qualifications, and particularly the Masters degree in Business Administration (MBA) from its level of 1,200 graduates a year in 1986 to a total of 10,000 by the year 2000. It was also envisaged that this expansion would be met by increased use of in-house and part-time MBAs, rather than through full-time study with its attendant problems of disrupting career continuity and management stability. A linked area of concern was to facilitate the acquisition of professional qualifications to provide evidence of rising standards of management competence. The present survey undertook to examine the extent to which private sector companies were offering assistance to their managerial employees, a particularly important aspect as so many respondents had indicated that they were experiencing difficulties in recruiting professional, technical and managerial staff. Company provision for MBA and professional qualification assistance is shown in Table 7.6.

Whilst no comparative figures are available, it does seem that companies are offering some practical assistance in financial and time terms to their managers to upgrade their managerial and (especially) professional qualifications. Nevertheless, half of responding companies offer no practical assistance for MBAs, a figure which escalates to 70 per cent for smaller companies, who may suffer a lack of awareness of the availability of advanced qualifications, or perceive a lack of utility of this qualification to small-firm executives; alternatively, these figures may simply help to confirm the severe time and financial pressures under which many managers in the small-firm sector operate.

Table 7.6: Company provision for advanced management qualifications

Provision	MBA (%)	Professional qualification (%)
Not at all	50	26
Pay all fees	7	15
Pay some fees	10	16
Time off	4	1
Finance for self study	3	5
Fees with time off	25	27
	N = 68	*N* = 88

Table 7.7: Annual allocations for formal management training

Management group	Average number of days (%)		
	0	*1–5*	*5+*
Senior Management	27	43	30
Middle Management	21	40	39
Supervisory	28	45	28

(*N* = 70)

With regard to management training, respondents were asked to detail the number of days training received by different management groups annually. Details are shown in Table 7.7. Again, a blend of optimism and pessimism emerges with about one-quarter of companies providing no managerial training at all, but rather more than a quarter offering in excess of five days annually. When we recall, for example, that proponents of the Management Charter Initiative were originally proposing a minimum level of five days off-the-job training for executives in 1987 (Handy 1987: 31), and the same author identified an average allocation of one day's training a year for managers in Britain (1988: 164), it appears that some com- panies are making progress. Details are shown in Table 7.8.

Also, on a positive note, 44 per cent of companies reported an increase in management training expenditure over the previous 12 months and more than half of large and over a third of medium-sized companies planned to increase their expenditure in the next 12 months. Main areas of anticipated increase were for training in human resource

Table 7.8: Five days or more formal training

Size of company	% of companies providing minimum five days training annually		
	Senior management	*Middle management*	*Supervisory*
Small	40	35	38
Medium	46	49	42
Large	60	80	70

management followed by business development and finance. Increases in expenditure over the last year were attributed largely to human resources, finance and to a lesser extent, new technology.

Whether the positive developments noted above amount to a comprehensive and permanent policy by companies to train their managers, or whether this was a temporary 'high' linked to good trading conditions, regular publicity about training and the signal of labour shortages is difficult to know. It should also be borne in mind that the funds allocated by companies for aggregate training expenditure were not high. Whilst the questionnaire did not ask respondents to quantify management training expenditure, it did ask them to state 'approximately what proportion of your training expenditure is allocated to management training or development' (see Table 7.9).

Table 7.9 shows that companies, many with already low training expenditures, tend not to invest large proportions of these sums (or many make little or no specific allocation) for the development of their managers. Nevertheless, the overall contours of the survey indicate that in larger companies at least, some positive training and developmental initiatives are being implemented for managers; whether these voluntary efforts will be sufficiently well-established to withstand the contractionist effects of a trade recession is difficult to assess. If past history is any guide, the answer must be negative.

COMPUTER SKILLS AND TECHNOLOGY TRAINING

The dimensions and pace of technological change have been well documented by Northcott (1986, in McLoughlin and Clark 1988: 23) and by

Table 7.9: Allocation of training expenditure on management training or development

Allocation (%)	No. of companies	Valid % of companies
Zero	16	22
1–15	17	24
16–30	13	18
31–45	3	4
46–60	15	21
61+	8	11
	72	100

Daniel in his analysis of the 1984 WIRS survey. The latter study found evidence of extensive introduction of 'new' microelectronics-based technology in British industry, and especially in large-scale manufacturing (Daniel 1987: 32). Technological progress has been occurring at an even greater pace in office work, where 'about one half of all workplaces employing non-manual workers had experienced . . . major change' (1987: 39).

Nevertheless, many commentators have pointed out that in technological terms, Britain is falling behind competitor countries. In 1985, for example, in Britain only 14,000 graduate engineers and technology students qualified, compared with 21,000 in Germany and 15,000 in France (Cassels 1990: 43). In addition, engineering and technological courses in France and Germany are of longer duration and of higher standard than their British equivalents (Prais 1989: 220).

To compound the problems of a 'technology gap', expenditure on research and development (R&D) in the UK is beginning to fall behind the pace set by other countries. In 1988 and 1989, governmental expenditure on R&D amounted to 2.3 per cent of national GDP, which places it fifth in the world research league. But one half of UK expenditure was accounted for through military and defence spending, a higher proportion than in comparable countries. Also, civil expenditure in these countries continues to increase, while Britain's remains static.

Technical and technological qualifications achieved throughout the occupational range tend to be fewer and of lower standard than those found in other countries (Steedman and Wagner 1987; Daly *et al.* 1985). NIESR researchers were able to summarise their findings as:

> our comparisons of production methods in the two countries (i.e. Britain and Germany) have made it clear that economic success in a competitive world increasingly relies on – and may even *require* – the use of technologically advanced machinery.
>
> (Steedman and Wagner 1987: 131, original emphasis)

It could be added that the use of such machinery will also require skilled manpower to manage and utilise technology to its fullest capability. In the light of these pressures, and recognising the deficiencies in training practice, the government-sponsored YTS was introduced, in particular in its two-year form, in order to meet technological challenges by providing high-quality training. It was with some surprise, therefore, that our survey showed extremely low inclination by employers to use YTS to provide skills appropriate for new technology.

The survey demonstrates, however, that many companies were exploiting some aspects of new technology. In terms of hardware, over half the companies (57 per cent) had introduced personal computers, which are suitable for a wide range of work environments. Central mainframes were reported by half the respondents. These can act as a central store for information and as part of a network system for personal computers found in one-third of enterprises.

Table 7.10: Company use of computer software

Software	% of companies
Office Automation	77
Finance Packages	76
Inventory Control/Stockholding	53
Personnel Records	36
Computer-aided Design	32
Production Control	29

(N = 101)

The use of computer software by responding companies is shown in Table 7.10. The table shows that use was concentrated in the areas of office automation and in finance, helping to reinforce Daniel's point about the pervasiveness of office automation (see also Webster 1990). It is possible that these areas receive early attention due to the incremental nature of change (i.e. introduction of word processor, facsimile machines, etc. on a gradual basis), whilst computerisation of stocks, personnel records and production control might require considerably greater initial investment in terms of cost, time and qualified personnel.

Just under half the companies (48 per cent) stated that they employ staff with specialised knowledge of computing or related fields. These staff had been obtained through a combination of training and specialised recruitment. Three-quarters of respondents claim to have concrete plans to increase the use of technology and computerisation over the next 12 months, mostly through retraining rather than through additional recruitment; this could be a reflection of the harder market prevailing for technical expertise. Interestingly, whilst 87 per cent of technological expanders aim to retrain, only 67 per cent have matching plans to increase computer training expenditure.

EMPLOYEE INVOLVEMENT IN TRAINING DECISIONS

One possible sign of the importance which companies attach to training as part of their employee management approach might be found in the extent of interaction between employees and their managers over training decisions. Interaction could take place at a number of levels and with varying levels of formality.

The depth of employee involvement could then be registered on twin scales of formality and collective input into decision-making, both of which help to measure the extent to which training decisions form part of the formal decision-making process with regard to employment issues within an organisation. Generally speaking, the more passive, informal and individualised the involvement of employees in any employment issue, the less likely it is to be embedded within the organisational decision-making structure and the less opportunities that employees might have to influence the direction and strengths of the processes involved.

At the individual and relatively informal level, the subject of training could be raised through the appraisal system by managers in their performance discussions with appraisees. Second, there might be more widespread, though still relatively informal, communication to employees of company training policies or intentions. Third, more formal consultation procedures between managers and employee representatives over training may be offered and, finally, there could be a measure of joint decision-making between management and employee representatives through collective bargaining. In the latter case, management would normally conduct their negotiations through union channels. The establishment of training committees to 'cover the whole range of training issues' and which are fully involved in company training decisions, is the declared aim of both TUC and many individual unions, though as yet, these represent a level of formality and depth of involvement rarely encountered in current practice (Labour Research Dept 1990: 8–10).

Comparatively little research has been undertaken in the area of union involvement in training decisions. This is possibly surprising because, as is well recognised, training is more likely to be found in larger companies than smaller ones and unions are more likely to have a presence in larger establishments in determining employee terms and conditions of employment (Millward and Stevens 1986: chapter 7). Nevertheless, *Training in Britain* found virtually no evidence of union influence upon employer training decisions (Training Agency 1989: 41) whilst the TUC considers that 'very rarely indeed are the employees themselves or their representatives involved in the (training) decisions' (1989: 11), despite the fact that 'a key union role will need to be played at enterprise and workplace level' if twin goals of securing quality and continuity of training are to be met (TUC 1990: 1).

A recent survey report, however, suggests that the spread of union involvement in training decisions may be greater than was previously thought. In the survey, nearly half of the union representatives of over 900 workplaces said that they were consulted by the employer over training decisions (30 per cent) or that training decisions were agreed between employer and unions (17 per cent) (Labour Research Dept 1990: 6).

In the present survey, a substantial majority (86 per cent) of employers claimed that they 'formally' discuss training plans with individual employees prior to implementation. It could be assumed that these would include many of the 78 per cent of respondents who replied that they have implemented systems of performance appraisal and in this framework discuss individual contributions in terms of developmental opportunities needed to achieve higher performance. Over half of the respondents (57 per cent) with computer technology considered that its introduction had been subject to discussions with employees or their representatives, largely in the form of informal discussion either at initial planning stage, prior to introduction or during implementation.

The management replies obtained in the present study with regard to generalised, unspecified collective involvement do not differ too widely from the responses from union representatives provided by the study reported above. In our study, 17 per cent of all respondents stated that company training plans are subject to formal negotiation with employee representatives and 25 per cent were said to communicate their training plans to employee representatives. As only 46 per cent of companies in the survey recognise trade unions for collective bargaining purposes, it is likely that some managers have taken a broad interpretation of the meaning of 'formal negotiation', which usually requires the presence of a union: nevertheless, the survey suggests that employees are collectively engaged in broad training decisions to a larger extent than estimated by earlier studies.

When we come to examine specific areas of training decision-making, however, evidence of union involvement begins to look less certain. Whilst 10 per cent of the *Bargaining Report* respondents claimed that unions were involved in 'agreements covering young workers' (Labour Research Dept 1990: 7), in only two (out of twenty-seven) cases did we find companies involved in the YTS who pay above the basic allowance provided to trainees, arriving at their decision through discussions with union representatives. Similarly, only 10 per cent of all respondents state the presence of a new technology agreement, though specific reference to training was included in most of this small number of agreements. And whilst over half of the respondents stated that they engage in *informal* discussion with employees or their representatives at the various stages of implementation for new technology, only a total of six companies gained negotiated agreement, five of these prior to its introduction and one during implementation. Not one company which recognised unions achieved a negotiated settlement for the introduction of new technology at the initial planning stage. Higher proportions (17 per cent at planning, 28 per cent prior to introduction and 22 per cent during implementation) of companies which have introduced new technology claim to consult with their employees during these three stages.

It seems, therefore, that whilst reported by substantial numbers of respondents, employee involvement tends to be located at an informal level or to take place on an individual or communicative basis, rather than through representative agreement-seeking procedures. Though the findings are not sufficiently detailed to be able to conclude that training involvement is not taken seriously by management, they do signal that opportunities for employees to exert control over the decision-making process or outcomes are confined largely to informal individual inputs, or to the limited opportunities provided through forms of advisory machinery. With few exceptions, it seems that existing arrangements would allow companies considerable freedom to adjust levels and directions of training provision without seeking collective employee endorsement of management intentions and actions.

THE SPECIAL CASE OF THE SMALL COMPANY[1]

Written off by the Bolton Report in 1971 as being in 'terminal decline', small companies have subsequently enjoyed considerable changes in fortune. The valuable patronage of a Conservative government has been extended to a small-firm sector which represents to the government a means of industrial regeneration, employment growth and a vehicle for promoting independence, individualism and dynamism. In short, the very essence of the 'enterprise culture' would be found and reproduced in a thriving small-firm sector. The Labour Party also has placed considerable faith in the generative qualities of the small-firm sector.

This endorsement is reflected in the progress of small companies over the past decade. Unfortunately, an accurate figure for the actual number of firms is hard to calculate; size criteria vary, though a number of studies make use of fifty employees as a cut-off point to distinguish small from medium-scale concerns.

Quantifying 'employees' can, however, prove difficult, as self-employed salespeople and drivers, for example, may sometimes be included as members of the employed workforce. Nevertheless, an estimate of 6 million employed in small firms has been given (Rainnie 1989: 2) and the Business Line survey calculated that there were 750,000 independent businesses in Britain employing fewer than fifty people (Hakim 1989: 32). Of these, more than one-third had been created in the years 1982–8 (Hakim 1989: 34). Net growth appears to have been sustained throughout the 1980s. It has been calculated that the number of surviving businesses grew by 10 per cent between 1980 and 1985 (Rainnie 1989: 2). Between 1980 and 1988 VAT registrations for companies grew by 17 per cent. According to Mayes and Moir, the majority of these new enterprises are likely to be small. Self-employment grew by 60 per cent over the same period (Mayes and Moir 1989: 15). A recent study showed that firms with less than twenty employees contributed a net gain of 290,000 jobs between 1985 and 1987, more than ten times the net creation rate of larger concerns (Gallagher et al. 1990: 92).

To complement the government's ideological backing, small firms also enjoy substantial practical support from the same source. Indirectly, small organisations are exempted from the provisions of certain employment regulations, in order not to deter employers in these companies from taking on or releasing staff. Part-time employment is especially common in smaller concerns, and these employees are required to serve longer periods in order to become eligible for employment protection. Exempting under-21-year-old employees from Wage Council regulations is expected to benefit the many small employers found in Wage Council industries.

As we saw in Chapter 2 the education system now also contributes actively to the encouragement of an enterprise culture through school-based work preparation programmes such as the Technical and Vocational Education Initiative, one aim of which is to emphasise 'initiative, motivation, enterprise and other areas of personal development' in 14–18-year-old participants. This programme is mirrored by the Higher Education Initiative designed to inject equivalent values into undergraduate studies. Direct government encouragement of small firms is provided by minimising tax and bureaucratic restrictions and through offering a range of government-sponsored services to small firms. The Enterprise Initiative and Small Firms Services provide advice for small and medium-sized concerns, whilst at local levels, financial and practical support is offered through Enterprise and Development Agencies. The Government has also introduced a scheme providing guaranteed loans to small business. In 1988–9 almost £65 million was offered in a total of 2,291 loans. In 1989, the Business Growth Training (BGT) programme was launched to provide a range of low-cost consultancy services designed to improve the effectiveness of training in small and medium-sized businesses.

Most importantly, the Training and Enterprise Councils (TECs) established in England and Wales and Local Enterprise Companies (LECs) in Scotland aim as a significant part of their responsibilities to 'promote the development of small businesses at the local level' (Employment for the 1990s, December 1988: 60). Eventually, TECs and LECs are expected to assume responsibility for most support services available to small and newly-established companies (*Employment Gazette*, March 1989: 112).

These various support agencies might be regarded as especially necessary owing to the high risks faced by small companies. In particular, they experience a high mortality rate in their early years, a 'propensity to die rather than contract' (Gallagher *et al*. 1990: 97). It has been estimated that more than 60 per cent of small firms fail within the first three years, adversely affecting the employment prospects of staff, as well as owners, leading Daniel to comment that: 'A striking feature of the characteristics of the unemployed was how disproportionately they were drawn from small establishments' (Daniel 1985, quoted in Rainnie 1989: 2). Continuing high interest rates combined with business rating changes implemented under recessionary conditions are likely to dramatically swell the numbers of small firm failures.

A second major problem facing small companies concerns growth. Many small independent organisations fail to develop, possibly because they do not possess the necessary management skills required to overcome the financial, market and human resource difficulties faced by many small employers contemplating expansion (Gallagher *et al*. 1990: 96; Mayes and Moir 1989: 26–31; Scottish Education Department 1986: 13–18; *Guardian*, 25 October 1989).

Considerable research activity has been directed at identifying small firm characteristics which would signal potential and capacity for growth and hence, 'targeting' for assistance; as yet, however, no firm conclusions have been drawn (Hakim 1989; Mayes and Moir 1989; Turok and Richardson 1989). A static company could have the effect of limiting employment security for existing employees in terms of its enhanced vulnerability to failure and would provide only replacement openings for new recruits; opportunities for personal advancement in static companies would also be severely restricted. The reality of the threats posed to employees by employment insecurity is demonstrated in a recent survey indicating that more small companies expected to lose labour than those anticipating an expansion in the first quarter of 1990 (*Financial Times*, 22 May 1990).

The small firm in Scotland

As all but one of the survey small firms operated exclusively within Scotland, regarded by many as a depressed economic region of Britain, it is worth considering whether there are any special features to the local economy which might effect small firm growth and development. Data for small firm activity in Scotland has been somewhat sparse, providing fertile ground for allegations of lack of native initiative and a preference for 'paternalistic, well-meaning bureaucracy'. Moreover, this preference for 'dependence' has 'retarded our economic growth and national self-confidence'. The prescribed remedy for Scottish society is a good dose of 'entrepreneurship, innovation and enterprise' (M. Rifkin, 1987, quoted in *Scottish Business Insider*, March 1990).

These assertions have been examined by Ashcroft and his colleagues in their comparative study of regional VAT registrations, in which Scotland trailed in eleventh place out of twelve British regions for the period 1980–6. This weak performance was distributed fairly uniformly throughout Scotland. Nevertheless, the authors found no evidence of a relationship between low rates of small firm formation and a 'dependency culture'. Rather, the pattern could be explained by a number of influences, which include: low levels of wealth as demonstrated by home ownership, under-representation in education, managerial and professional skills and by an unfavourable plant structure in which small plants are somewhat under-represented in the Scottish economy (Ashcroft *et al.* 1989).

Further recent findings demonstrate that the *employment* effects of Scottish new firm formation have been less than those found for the UK as a whole: an estimated 21,400 jobs might have been generated by 1986 if the UK employment effect of small firm formation were to be applied to Scotland (Standing Commission on the Scottish Economy 1989: 28).

Training and the small firm

In light of the above, training becomes a vital issue for all small firms but most especially in economically subdued areas like Scotland. For employees, training is important not only in order to optimise work performance but for the opportunities it provides to extend work capability: in the event of firm failure, skills should be transferable to other employment contexts, thereby minimising risks of subsequent sustained unemployment. Nevertheless, for small firms to consolidate and grow in stable fashion requires their owners and managers to acquire managerial qualities which supplement their entrepreneurial abilities. Most commentators agree that managerial capabilities can be enhanced through training and development (Handy *et al.* 1988; Constable and McCormick 1987). An important part of the present enquiry was to establish the levels and directions of management development and training provided by Scottish-based small companies.

Respondents were asked to specify the amounts of training expenditure allocated to these activities. We saw above that in aggregate, 22 per cent of companies make no specific allocation of funds for management training: Table 7.11 shows the proportions of companies for each size category stating that no specific allocations were made to management training. The table confirms that nearly half of small companies replying to the question were unable to specify any allocation of training expenditure to their management. One interpretation of this is that small companies simply do not disaggregate their expenditures, though the question did ask for *approximate* rather than detailed allocations.

Table 7.11: Respondents reporting zero training allocations to managers

	%	
Small	42	(*N* = 26)
Medium	15	(*N* = 26)
Large	5	(*N* = 19)

Our doubts are strengthened, however, by the modest proportion (15 per cent) of small companies reporting that expenditure on management training had increased over the previous 12 months, in contrast with the 46 per cent and 69 per cent of medium and larger companies who reported increases. Further, only 15 per cent of small companies had intentions to increase expenditure over the next year, compared with 28 per cent of medium and 56 per cent of large companies.

Management development is often pursued through gaining higher management qualifications. Almost all (96 per cent) large companies and 73 per cent of medium ones make some contribution, financial and/or in terms of time, for managers to gain professional qualifications, whilst a half of small companies make no contribution whatsoever. This figure increased to 70 per cent of small companies making no contribution for managers studying for the premium management qualification, the MBA (compared with 59 per cent of medium and 28 per cent of large companies).

With the majority of MBA students recruited from large organisations, and with much of the MBA syllabus relevant to larger-scale corporate requirements, it could be contended that such a qualification has little relevance for the needs of smaller concerns. Equally, it could be considered that the time and expense required to gain such a qualification, whether through part-time or distance study, again mitigates against smaller employer participation. In such cases, it might be anticipated that shorter courses for managers would find more favour among smaller organisations. However, when asked about short course participation, a similar pattern emerges: two-thirds of small company respondents replied that internally provided short courses were never offered by their companies (compared with 'never' response of 27 per cent in medium companies and 5 per cent in large). Externally provided short courses fared somewhat better, though not one small company respondent reported their provision on a regular basis (compared with 24 per cent and 33 per cent reported for medium and large companies respectively). Nevertheless, more than one-third (39 per cent) of small companies reported never using external course providers at all (9 per cent medium; 6 per cent large).

Training for employees

Small firms have been characterised as a 'sector notoriously resistant to training' (*Guardian*, 27 June 1988). The present survey does little to dispel such notions. The study shows that the majority of senior trainers in the thirty-seven small companies were senior members of the management/ownership team, but two-thirds of them lacked any qualification relevant to training or personnel management. The multiple responsibilities of these managers were demonstrated by the finding that

84 per cent spent less than one-tenth of their time on training issues, and as training when provided in small companies tends to be informal, 'in-house' and specific to company needs, it suggests very little concentrated attention paid to employee training by small firm employers.

Unlike larger companies, smaller concerns tend not to have an identifiable budget for training (82 per cent did not, compared with 44 per cent and 21 per cent of medium and large companies). An indication of the limits of small firm expenditure on training can be gauged from the finding that virtually all the companies spent less than £5,000 per annum on training activities. Though small companies over-all were less likely to engage in 'in-house' training than larger concerns, one-third of small companies allocated more than three-quarters of their training expenditure to internal training despite an overall lack of training expertise and within the limited budget constraints shown above; a further quarter spent an equivalent amount on the services of external consultants. Small firms were far less likely than larger ones to use educational establishments (59 per cent spent nothing in this area) or government-sponsored training (84 per cent spent nothing), suggesting that few trainees in small companies are undertaking the formal training which might enhance their attractiveness in the external labour market.

Low-scale expenditure by small firms might not be considered a problem because of the availability of low-cost government and local initiative training support. However, our findings show that small companies are less likely than larger firms to participate in governmental schemes; only 39 per cent participated in the Youth Training Scheme (YTS) and use of the government-backed Employment Training (ET) was confined to two of the thirty-seven small companies. Almost all small company non-participants in ET had also not been involved in earlier government schemes for adults.

SUMMARY

The debate on employer commitment to training has recently intensified following the government's decision to transfer the bulk of training responsibilities to employer-orientated LECs and TECs. Critics argue that since employers have rarely shown much in the way of commitment to training, to reward them by offering control over training finance and policy is both self-defeating and cynical. The government's Secretary for Employment, in return, contends that employers are now: 'heavily committed to training, and that their investment is rising . . . . Employers are investing in skills not because they are compelled to, but because they see advantage to their businesses of doing so' (Reported in the *Guardian*, 15 December 1990).

Support for this argument rests largely upon the *Training in Britain* findings that employers spent £18 billion on their training activities in 1986/7, figures strongly disputed by opposition spokespersons who claim far smaller levels of training expenditure: one report suggests that annual training expenditure, exclusive of pay, varies from a low of £32 annually per employee in the distribution sector to £159 in banking, finance and insurance, in total barely reaching a tenth of the amounts identified by *Training in Britain*. The same report concludes that Britain's crisis in training is being maintained by employer reluctance to train and by government cuts in training support expenditure (McLeish 1990).

Our survey figures incline to the pessimistic end of both the expenditure and investment orientation spectrum, with direct training costs per employee averaging from £73 in small companies to £111 in larger ones. In the distributive trades sector, seven out of fifteen companies (47 per cent) spent less than £50 annually on training each employee, uncomfortably close to the 1988 Labour Cost Survey average figure of £32 per head cited by McLeish. Our study offered few signs that government schemes were incorporated into company training activities, let alone formulated as part of investment training plans: YTS was used principally for recruitment or even altruistic purposes, but rarely was its use acknowledged as a means to remove skill shortages and even more rarely was it used as a platform for high-skill technological work.

There were, however, some favourable findings in our survey. Overall expenditure on training was said to have increased, particularly among larger concerns and a substantial majority of these respondents expected to make further increases in the coming year, though the looming recession may place these plans in jeopardy. In particular, companies seem to be paying more attention to the development of their managers, though within a generally modest training expenditure framework. Coupled with unambitious expenditures for new technology training and an absence of formal collective employee involvement in training decisions, these low expenditure patterns do little to suggest that a revolution in British management practice has occurred with regard to training, especially in smaller firms where the deficiencies are even more pronounced.

Small and independent companies are expected to be the mainspring of economic growth. Whilst substantial State assistance has been made available to stimulate small firm formation, the extent to which these companies can grow and flourish without regular injections of employee training and especially, of management development, is questionable. Whilst training opportunities currently exist for small companies, the extent to which these are used is limited.

The survey shows that very few small companies undertake the managerial training which might endorse the entrepreneurial flair of their founders with managerial skills needed for organisational consolidation and stability which might help smaller companies to survive during periods of economic uncertainty and recession.

Of equal concern is the lack of attention given to employee training. At a time when skill shortages are already apparent and the implications of demographic change well-recognised, resources allocated to training in small companies are not high. Unemployment is again beginning to increase and it is sadly inevitable that many job losses will emanate from small companies; training dislodged labour may not be seen by small employers as their direct concern, but it certainly is in the interests of the affected employees and of the State. It is to these points of contested interests, which lay perhaps at the heart of the entire training debate, that we turn in the concluding chapters.

Chapter 8

A way forward?
The market approach

Simply investing in new technology or systems guarantees nothing. Without education and training, the potential benefits are never achieved. You can not buy productivity, it has to be earned by training and investment in people . . . . Why does the world have to learn time and time again that the investment with the best return is education and training?

(Hinchcliffe 1990, quoted in Crewe 1991)

INTRODUCTION

The final two chapters present and assess two contrasting policy approaches for raising the levels of training in Britain. The first, representing government policy in Britain over the past ten years is a market-driven approach heavily reliant for its operation upon the voluntary actions of employers and employees. The second, appraised in further depth in the final chapter, considers the potential scope for a more government-centred strategy. Before contemplating prospective ways forward for training in Britain it is worthwhile first to contextualise the debate by briefly summarising the principal issues identified in preceding chapters.

The opening chapter proposed that performance productivity, which unites a concern for output with quality and product development, has emerged as a major focus for product and service competitiveness. There are signs that the importance of performance and the means to achieve higher levels are becoming registered with employers in Britain. Conversely, there is very little evidence that, through their activities, unions have attempted to frustrate managerial efforts to improve performance through opposing the introduction of new technology or by other means.

Recent government actions towards employment relations reform were reviewed in Chapter 2, which concluded that despite the lack of evidence of union constraints on employer initiatives, government reforms have sought to reduce collective influence at work through encouraging labour market individualism. A competitive education system sensitive to labour market demands was introduced with similar intentions.

Chapter 3 demonstrated that the same motivations were evident in manpower policy, where voluntarism combined with market regulation has provided the mainspring of State action. This approach was reflected in the decisions of government to allow training at work to be subject principally to the individual decisions of employers and employees, and subsequently sharpened through the introduction of TECs and LECs in support of this aspiration.

Chapter 4 showed that education has become a priority objective for comparatively industrialised countries, which have also developed sophisticated vocational education programmes. With the possible exception of Japan (which nevertheless, has developed its manpower by utilising school-acquired theoretical knowledge as a basis for more applied approaches offered by employers), a high State profile in formulating and guiding training and vocational education has been the rule rather than the exception. There is little doubt that the high levels of economic performance enjoyed by these countries are directly attributable to educational and training factors.

With so much emphasis placed in Britain upon voluntary employer responsibility for training and in making the operation of manpower policy contingent upon their willing participation, Chapter 5 examined the ways in which employers have responded to these responsibilities. The overall conclusions, derived from a range of studies conducted in the mid-1980s, were that employer training efforts were marked by complacency and short-term considerations.

Chapter 6 used empirical material to explore the nature of any changes in employer practices which might have occurred by the end of the decade. The survey and other evidence found that training was still very much treated as a 'minority' activity by managers, including personnel.

Chapter 7 further confirmed this lowly status by showing that actual expenditure on training was low in most companies surveyed, and found few signs to suggest that training matters were being included as part of any pattern of strategic management.

POSSIBLE DIRECTIONS FOR EDUCATION AND TRAINING

There is a clear and direct relationship between economic performance and education and training performance. The potential effects of this relationship become tangible in the short-term when current employer activities are visibly constrained through 'skill shortages'. The CBI reported that compared with 1982, when 2.5 per cent of companies expected skill shortages to hamper output, by 1988, the proportion had risen to 20 per cent. In the high-technology Thames Valley area, 84 per cent of manufacturing enterprises were reporting production difficulties attributable to shortages of skills (*Financial Times*, 8 December 1988).

In the longer term, shortages of scientific, engineering and technological professionals jeopardise the pace of industrial development and production. We saw in Chapter 4 that Britain is *currently* facing a shortfall of 8,000 qualified engineers and the signs are that this gap is set to widen in the future. Research and development crucial for technological advancement also becomes jeopardised by these skill deficiencies, a problem highlighted by the House of Lords Select Committee on Science and Technology in 1989: ˋ

> All the United Kingdom's plans for civil R&D are at risk from one factor, manpower shortages . . . These factors, combined with demographic change which will cut the working population, make a shortage of skilled staff a certainty, unless remedial action is taken soon.
>
>   (Reported in Association of University Teachers 1989)

Few observers of the economic scene would dispute that major steps need to be taken to reform education and training in Britain in order to help fulfil the country's economic performance potential. The urgency of this task is made more apparent not only by the educational and training achievements already secured by the governments and employers of our trading partners but by their projected aims for expansion in the future.

With this consensus of opinion, it is also not surprising that the reform packages offered by the parties with a major and direct interest in Britain's economic performance display broadly general agreement over the desired directions for education and training reform. Hence, all major contributors have acknowledged that post-compulsory education participation rates must improve radically and quickly, if they are to be brought up to the full-time education continuation rates of Japan (92 per cent), USA (94 per cent), France (78 per cent) and Germany (69 per cent); that access to higher education must be opened out without compromising standards; and that more efficient delivery systems for training in industry must be developed.

The means proposed to fulfil these attainments differ, however, according to the ideological and political perspectives of the prospective reformers. Basically, two models for reform can be identified, one which emphasises the efficiency of market forces to create and allocate the skills required to service the economy and an alternative view which argues for greater levels of planning and State direction in these processes. Both approaches have powerful advocates, who through their actions at the political and industrial level, could influence the progress of any strategy adopted. For these reasons, the recommendations offered by the principal proponents of these policy options deserve careful consideration.

THE MARKET APPROACH

Earlier chapters demonstrated that the Conservative government has pledged to raise performance through revitalising market forces, as reflected in its educational reforms, through its employment relations policies and in its advocacy of training voluntarism, realised through the establishment of locally-based TECs and LECs as the main instruments for shaping the delivery of training.

In *Towards a Skills Revolution* (1989)[1] the CBI has also formulated a comprehensive set of proposals which reflect the concern which it, and its members, feel toward the problems of skill deficiencies. Interestingly, diagnosis of problems differs little from that of the TUC considered below, and in its educational recommendations that half of the relevant age group attain NVQ III level or its academic equivalent of two 'A' level passes and five good GCSE passes, similar, if slightly less ambitious, objectives are sought.

In recent years, the influence of the CBI with regard to government policy over workplace training and development has undoubtedly grown and a number of government initiatives have emerged from CBI-originated proposals.[2] For this reason, in tandem with consideration of the merits of the ideas presented, it is important to consider the blueprint offered by the CBI. With regard to training and employment, the CBI wishes to see the elimination of any employment not associated with 'structured education and training leading to recognised qualifications' (1989: 19) for 16–18-year-olds and calls upon all involved parties to voluntarily work towards this attainment. Removal of non-training employment would be effected through provision of individual training credits which would empower trainees not only 'with greater control over their own development' but over non- training employers as well; with credits in their hands, 'young people in short supply would simply go to other employers offering training' (1989: 24).

These initiatives are complemented by proposals to encourage employers to become 'investors in training', which would involve incorporation of training plans into business plans, setting training targets and budgets, evaluation of training expenditure, provision of support for employee self-development, and furnishing details of training activity to corporate stakeholders such as managers, employees, investors and shareholders in company annual reports. Responsibility for encouraging companies to become 'investors' is delegated to TECs by the CBI proposals.

There is no doubt that the CBI has given considerable and committed thought both to the problems faced by the country and to potential solutions. Nevertheless, the critical importance of the issue for future economic progress demands that recommendations and the assumptions upon which they rest be subjected to close scrutiny; the accumulating skills crisis demonstrates that the country cannot afford to carry mistakes forward.

One weakness in the CBI approach is that it assumes considerable community of interest between employer and employee/trainee; indeed, in places both parties appear to be regarded as an homogeneous prospective customer entity with little distinction between their needs. Elsewhere, however, training credits are recommended on the basis that trainee/employees are the sole customer, with employers seen as intermediaries between them and suppliers, or as the suppliers themselves. For example, the CBI has enthusiastically welcomed the proposals for TECs as laid down in the 'Employment for the 1990s' White Paper, which stated that through TECs, 'government hope to place 'ownership" of the training and enterprise system where it belongs – with employers' (1989).

In other words the trainee/employees are expected to 'buy' training from their employer/owners. Under these circumstances, at the very least, there is likely to be tension between the parties over the content and nature of training offered. Employers, particularly when operating in tight local labour markets, if they train at all (and there is no external pressure exerted upon them to do so in the CBI proposals), will wish to provide specific training designed to bind the trainee to the employer, rather than furnish footloose trainees with the general skills which would encourage free exercise of their mobility. On the other hand, trainees benefit from accumulating general, portable and formal skill qualifications. There is, then, no automatic guarantee that employer and employee interests will coincide, especially when labour is in short supply.

This problem is compounded by the danger that employers will wish training to be supplied in response to employer-designated short-term and localised skill shortages. Indeed, TECs will operate on the basis of providing nationally recognised qualifications which are appropriate through their adaptability to meet local needs, as defined by employers (1989: 42). Under these circumstances, it is difficult to envisage the ways by which individual young trainees will gain 'greater control over their own development'.

If anything, control over trainees is likely to be vested in the employers, who, under the proposals, would be expected to record and maintain the 'achievements' of individual trainees once they had left school and entered a traineeship as first-time employees. Indeed, the CBI envisages that 'employers will need to maintain the Individual Action Plan during the early years of a young person's employment and throughout working life' (1989: 23). This raises questions of control, not only over training, but over individual prospects of employment and would seem to locate influence rather firmly in the hands of the employer, who will understandably wish to satisfy immediate output needs. Unless employers start to adopt longer time horizons for their other mainstream activities, it seems rather fanciful to assume that they will start acting in this way in the very area which they have constantly and consistently neglected. In the absence of representation from other, educational and employment, interests, there is a very real danger that this approach will simply replicate, and potentially reinforce, current short-term trends. Why should employers encourage, voluntarily, the long-term general development of employees for whom there is no guarantee of long-term use?

Indeed, all the recommendations addressed to employers seek for voluntary action by them to increase skill levels. Infused throughout the whole report is a belief that somehow the market and its voluntarist derivatives can be made to work by a magical formula through which exhortation and employer self-interest will help to link employer interests with those of employees and with those of the nation as a whole. Unfortunately, as we have seen time and time again, there is no guarantee that employer interests do or will coincide with those of individual employees or with the government's understandable concern to provide a wider skills base, particularly as in all other areas of commercial activity, short-term interests remain paramount.

It is clear, as stated at the beginning of the chapter, that the national overall interest is best served through raising continuation rates for young people entering post-compulsory education and hence their progression into higher education. Higher level skill shortages in science, technology and engineering have dogged British commercial performance for years, and yet the market has failed to resolve the crisis. Moreover, projected changes in the demand for labour point towards further growth in the need for technological and professional occupations (Training Agency 1989: 73). Will future calls for these occupations be met through a market mechanism or is a more planned and participative approach, involving all major stakeholders, a more viable option to take? The capacity to participate in higher education is a potentially long-term benefit which can offer genuine control to individuals over their future development, but over which the CBI report is unfortunately muted.[3]

It is also clear that although the CBI appears to hitch its flag firmly to the mast of voluntarism and to market relations, some doubts remain: from beneath the rhetoric surfaces an occasional acknowledgement that market forces alone are unlikely to bring about the 'skills revolution' called for by the CBI. The Confederation calls for the employer-dominated TECs to act as the 'market regulator' of training. Why employers should be called upon to regulate a market which is supposed to be self-regulating is something of a puzzle in conceptual terms, though as a mechanism for training delivery to employers, it becomes more understandable. To this query can be added the perceptive observation made by Cassels that the success of the proposals to eliminate all under-18 employment which is not accompanied by recognised formal training is dependent upon 'young people, educationalists, Government, unions and employers' coming together 'to help make it happen' (1990: 19). Cassels rightly points out that this 'is a remarkable suggestion coming from a source so dedicated to market solutions' (1990: 32).

Throughout this book, the credibility of a market-based approach has become increasingly undermined by the weight of evidence arraigned against it, and at this summarising stage, it is contended that on at least three counts, a pure or heavily market-oriented strategy should be approached with scepticism. First, the evidence of ten years of market-led manpower policy offers precious little support to the efficacy of a market approach to training. Further, as was shown in earlier chapters, there are few signs that other countries have moved or are intending to move, in this direction. Finally, the many weaknesses observed in practice become all too apparent when considered at the conceptual level.

THE OBSERVED FAILURE OF A MARKET APPROACH TO INCREASE TRAINING

Whilst conceptually it can be argued that market forces are ill-equipped to lay down the foundations for the longer-term construction of training, empirical studies enable us to examine any shorter-term employer responses to the freedoms offered to them.

The numerous research findings outlined in Chapter 5 detailed Britain's failure to train in the mid-1980s in the midst of the flowering of governmental voluntarist and market-led policies. This is not the first time that attempts to manoeuvre market forces in support of training provision has been found wanting. Fairley has considered and evaluated an earlier market-led approach to skills acquisition, re-introduced in the boom period following the end of the Second World War, after wartime regulatory controls which had increased the amount of attention given to training had been dismantled (Sheldrake and Vickerstaffe 1987: 25):

> This (voluntary) system failed to produce adequate supplies of skilled manpower in the 1950s when the economy was expanding and industry was much more competitive than it is today.
>
> (Fairley 1981: 164)

The survey findings presented in Chapters 6 and 7 tend to confirm that in the aftermath of the 1980s, following ten full years of reliance upon market-led forces supported by considerable government exhortation, there are few signs that skill shortages are being remedied or that employers are voluntarily taking training steps which address these problems, especially for the long term.

In particular, we found only low levels of stated expenditure by employers on training, ranging from £73 a year in small companies to £111 in large ones. These expenditures occurred at a time of profitable trading and (possibly misplaced) optimism for future prospects; under conditions, according to the CBI, when employer inclinations toward training are most likely to be positive: 'Employers are ready and willing to respond to this challenge. As profitability has improved they have already stepped up their training performance' (CBI 1989: 17). It was also a time when over half of the sizeable minority or respondents reporting difficulties in recruiting skilled, technical, professional and managerial staffs pointed to shortages of available skills as the prime problem. If, as the *Training in Britain* study suggested, British industry tends to train as a response to immediate pressures, and if we assume skill shortages do present considerable pressures to companies in terms of immediate lost orders and longer term deficiencies in competitive capability, we can only speculate what the levels of training provision might be under less stressful conditions.

The survey also found that 40 per cent of companies with training budgets vary these in accordance with profit or performance levels. Whilst the appearance of budgets is in itself a welcome sign of attention to training matters, it would appear that these companies still tend to see and treat training as an *outcome* from profits rather than a major contributor to them, a tendency among British managers identified by Coopers & Lybrand in their earlier study and apparently (if not consciously) ratified by the CBI quote above.

The tendency of employers to vary their training expenditure according to trading conditions is neither a universal nor an immutable law. In Japan, for example, the biggest increase in training expenditure in manufacturing companies, 20 per cent over the previous year, occurred in 1975, a time of zero growth and when many sectors experienced an actual fall in output. In Dore and Sako's words: 'Japanese firms do not respond to recession by cutting training budgets, but by putting surplus man hours to improving skill levels' (1989: 80).

Training provision in small companies, as might be expected, showed little reaction to the stimulus of unleashed market forces. These companies are close to both customers and product market and most are engaged in a serious struggle for survival, as the high mortality rate of small companies shows. They are very much part of the market system. Yet without reasonable access to resources for training and development, as are available, for example, to small German companies, and with no requirement upon them to utilise the services of a Master craft worker for training as is also required in Germany, or legal compulsion to spend on training as occurs in France, the training record of small British companies does not appear to have been greatly improved through the operation of market forces.

Finally, little evidence was found to suggest that the status of training or of trainers had become elevated by the end of the decade. There was evidence, substantiated by other research findings, that personnel as an occupation has risen in its standing over the past few years, possibly as a consequence of organisational attempts to come to terms with their 'human resource' issues. The extent to which training has penetrated into these developments is much less certain, particularly in the light of MacKay and Torrington's findings that personnel tend to avoid involvement with training issues.

PRACTICE IN OTHER COUNTRIES

The experience of other countries shows that it is unusual for governments to rely primarily upon voluntary actions of the participants as a means to promote training. It is true that Japanese employers are under no compulsion to train, but maintaining a systematic linkage between education and industry has become an established feature of government policy into which Japanese employers contribute through their subsequent training activities. The managing director of Sumitomo Electric Industries put this integrative approach into context: 'Parents, schools and universities all contribute. We do the rest' (quoted in the *Financial Times*, 3 December 1990).

Preceding chapters have shown that Germany and France both rely upon a combination of legislation, manpower planning and joint regulation to stimulate and buttress employer training activities. Recent developments indicate that this pluralist approach is tending to grow rather than diminish. In France, a new law was passed in July 1990 extending the right of the provision of an individual training plan leading to a vocational qualification to all workers. This provision was incorporated into the legal rights of employees following a collective agreement made earlier in 1990 (*European Industrial Relations Review*, September 1990: 6).

CONCEPTUAL WEAKNESSES OF A MARKET-BASED APPROACH

There are two major difficulties in relying principally on the market as an instrument to satisfy skill requirements. First, there is no guarantee of co-ordination between the different contributors, notably the buyers and sellers, to product and labour market activity and, second, the market is not an effective mechanism for predicting or satisfying longer-term needs.

These weaknesses derive from the observation that we live and work in an uncertain and shifting world; the depth and duration of economic recessions cannot be forecast with any degree of precision and neither can their causes; changes in product markets through environmental or other global factors such as war-induced oil crises, cannot be predicted.

Competition emerges from other countries (e.g. Eastern Europe) with little warning. Internal factors can be equally problematic. The impact of technology is hard to assess; economists are still debating whether micro-chip technology is a net contributor to employment or to unemployment and whether new technology demands greater skill inputs to work or systematically strips employee discretion from work in a process of deskilling.

Under conditions of such uncertainty, it is perhaps not too surprising that a non-interventionist stance which is reliant upon employer and labour force responses to circumstances which may have little observable or immediate impact upon them does little to alleviate skill shortages, let alone prompt the parties to anticipate and respond to future ones. Such an approach can only contribute to growing disjunctures between individual employer actions and collective national need. Even when the impact might be anticipated, uncertainty may well inhibit employers from taking any action which is not immediately defensive. It will be recalled that the 1985 Coopers & Lybrand study found that environmental uncertainty was not conducive for companies to adopt a strategic perspective for training. It could be added, moreover, that macro-economic problems call for macro-economic levels of treatment. Training on its own, especially when dictated by narrow and short-term imperatives, cannot solve the problems arising from changes in the wider environment.

The recession of the early 1980s hit Britain with particular severity because the country lacked an effective mechanism to cope with the changes brought in its wake; the best that could be offered was an attempt to make an imperfectly functioning labour market operate more smoothly through removing identified 'impediments', and to offer employment palliatives to the worst-hit, highly visible and politically most sensitive groups to be affected by unemployment, namely young people.

The substantive differences between national longer-term requirements and the short-term demands of employers is one crucial factor in explaining the weakness of the market as a means of skill resource allocation. Reliance upon the market *may* satisfy labour requirements raised through short-term pressures and as experienced by employers. Government policy which concentrates on satisfying these demands runs the risk of responding primarily to temporary localised employer signals, whilst not dealing comprehensively with the broader long-term requirements of a dynamic economy operating within a broader national or supra-national context.

Moreover, the labour market itself suffers imperfections as an allocative mechanism; delays and complexities of transmission, the relative immobility of labour, inadequate identification of needs and a suspicion of the principles of manpower forecasting and avoidance of its application are supplemented by a serious problem. Employers are loathe to commit funds for training purposes, especially if skills can be bought in or if the employer concentrates on low-skill, low-quality, low-added-value markets where products and services could be maintained at a low level of sophistication. This approach avoids capital investment and labour skill expenditure and helps to maintain a cycle described by Finegold and Soskice as the 'low-skills equilibrium' trap (1988: 22). There are other incompatibilities: labour is a factor of production derived from the existing product market. Possible developments in technology and demography will not be of prime concern to individual employers, who want labour specific to their operational requirements. So on the one hand, economic demands will be for flexible, transferable, high-quality skills, on the other, employers are wanting immediate enterprise-specific skills which are not easily transferable.

These issues also influence the responses of actual or potential employees, who along with government and employers, represent the third group of participants in the training equation. Under conditions of widespread uncertainty, there is little encouragement for them to undertake training, especially if this uncertainty is transmitted as insecurity in the work situation. In insecure conditions, people may contemplate training in order to escape from a threatening work situation, in which case little support might be forthcoming from the employer. This lends credence to the proposition that all three interested parties to skills may have different motives and priorities in acquiring skills.

We pointed out earlier that all governments concern themselves with the educative process, partly as an essential ingredient of fundamental democratic rights, partly for the transmission and progression of cultural and societal norms and partly as a means toward economic proficiency. We have seen that many of Britain's competitor countries have developed education systems which attach equal importance to academic education and its vocational and training branches. In other words, there is a strong argument for treating training as a specific form of education. If we take this view, short-term market criteria and reliance upon employers and their demands are unsuitable and unstable vehicles for the promotion of the long-term, consistent approach to training so long deficient in Britain. In short, if training is to be part of education, and not *vice versa*, as current governmental practice appears to advocate, then government needs to adopt a radically different approach, emphasising the educative potential of training, and to provide funding and supervision of standards to match those offered to academic disciplines. By no means does this imply that other parties to the education–industry interface should be denied access to policy-making; in fact, the opposite should be the case. The MSC was at its most effective when acting as a genuine tripartite body; but consensus needs to be replicated at all levels of education and industrial relations policy-making, which assumes a genuinely participative role both for trade unions and employers at workplace level, guided and advised by successive tiers of government-funded multi-partite bodies.

The conclusion that a market-led approach fails to prepare the interested parties adequately for long-term needs has been raised also by the Henley Centre with regard to urban planning and development; and the conclusions are uncomfortably similar; rather than encourage innovation, participation and efficient resource allocation, the free market fosters secrecy, short-term solutions to long-standing problems and a lack of community involvement over major decisions which affect peoples' everyday lives (Kellner 1990). Much the same argument can be made for decisions over one of the primary life-choice decisions in which all people have a stake, a decision which literally determines quality of life as consumer, producer and citizen: the extent and availability of education.

Chapter 9

A way forward?

Government intervention

THE INTERVENTIONIST ROUTE TO TRAINING

If the voluntary approach has failed to raise the levels of training in Britain to match those of our trading partners, and looks unlikely to succeed in the future, what are the possibilities that these aims might be achieved by an alternative route, through closer government association with the planning and delivery of training?

It will be recalled that previous government attempts to raise the quantity and quality of training through the intermediary of Industrial Training Boards gained precious little sympathy from industry. Employers resented paying a training levy and the scheme received a mixed response from unions, favourable from those representing lesser skilled workers who could stand to gain from a broader distribution of training arrangements but more hesitant from craft unions who suspected that their occupational privileges, based upon restricted access to apprenticeship training, would be eroded.

Despite operating with only grudging support and amid constant criticism of their activities, it should be remembered that following their introduction in 1964 the Boards did contribute to raising both the profile and the amount of training provided through the 1960s. Between 1964 and 1968, the numbers of workers who received training increased by 15 per cent, with at least part of this growth attributable to the Boards' activities. In particular, some individual Boards reported considerable growth in numbers undergoing training. The Engineering Industry Training Board estimated that between 1966/7 and 1969/70 there had been 50 per cent growth in numbers trained in that industry (Woodhall 1974: 80; Lees and Chiplin 1970). Numbers of training personnel increased and there was virtual unanimity that training quality had also shown marked improvement. Despite its misgivings about government involvement in company affairs, the CBI was moved to comment that: 'What the Act has clearly done is to transform the whole climate of opinion and concentrate far more informed attention on training in British industry. This may prove to be its greatest benefit so far' (CBI 1971, reported in Woodhall 1974: 82).

Mindful that attempts to bring about the substantial improvements needed to bolster Britain's performance productivity through government intervention relies upon gaining industrial support for its eventual success, both the Labour Party (in 1990) and TUC (in 1989) have put forward vocational education and training policy proposals which link an active role for the State with a measure of autonomy for the principal participants as the chosen means for raising standards of training provision and delivery.

In its reform proposals, outlined in 1990 in the policy document *Investing in Britain's Future*, the Labour Party focuses attention on the shortcomings of present educational arrangements for 16–19-year-olds with a staged package aimed both at progressively increasing the rates of full-time educational participation beyond the age of 16 and at improving its content across the ability range. The document proposes that by the end of the decade, all young people should expect to continue in education and training to the age of 18, beyond which they will be entitled to gain additional qualifications by progressing to more advanced forms of education, or by receiving training backed by formal qualifications.

Higher levels of education would be achieved through the establishment of a national level Education Standards Council (ESC) whose function would be to monitor and endorse targets set by each local education authority (LEA) to expand participation. Each LEA would also specify the means by which it expects to meet its progressively increasing participation rate. The ESC would agree a national budget and organise its allocation among LEAs according to their agreed budgeted needs. Other reforms would include financial support for low income families to encourage continued participation and the introduction of common core subjects into a post-16 curriculum which would be widened in order to prevent over-early specialisation.

Initial training following post-compulsory education would shift away from its present inferior status toward qualifications-backed vocational education through the introduction of a four-year traineeship, primarily education based for the first two years and more work-based for the remaining two years. The traineeship would be linked directly to the new post-16 curriculum, and would thereby offer access to higher education. The origins of this approach can be traced to the German dual system considered in Chapter 4.

Like the Labour Party, the TUC acknowledges the harm done to young people and to the economy alike by the institutionalised and persistent subordination of vocational education to academic studies. It further recognises that there have been a number of obstacles to the development of vocationally orientated education in Britain and that genuine training progress can only be built into education when these obstacles are removed. These obstacles include: the tendency of an educational establishment to cling to the elitist status quo; a confusing mixture of vocational qualifications with varying degrees of rigour and often with little obvious connection between them, thereby offering restricted opportunity for progression; barriers to gaining access to education for disadvantaged groups such as the unemployed, older workers and women. Like the Labour proposals, the TUC calls for the establishment of organic links which encourage continuity and progression between educational study, qualifications and work-related training.

The aims of the TUC have been set out in a strategy statement, *Skills 2000* (TUC 1989). To overcome access disadvantages, the TUC proposes four major rights to training for individuals. These rights cover the following areas:

A right to quality training and retraining to ensure skill progression, and paid educational leave.

A right to choice in training regardless of sex, age, sexual orientation, religion or disability, and regardless of the job performed or the hours worked.

A right to take part in decisions about what training would be most effective.

A right to nationally and internationally recognised standards of training.

(TUC 1989: 6)

There would be little disagreement over this set of broad principles. The major question involves how they would be implemented. To meet these proposed entitlements, the TUC (like the CBI) argues for an individual 'record of achievement' for all school pupils under a broad curriculum covering vocational and academic study; the provision of education and training credits for post-16 study; rationalisation by the NCVQ of academic and vocational qualifications in order to promote opportunities for vertical and horizontal development for people at work. French-style paid educational leave for individual employees should eventually be on offer. A training support system available to unemployed people on a voluntary basis is recommended. Finally, the TUC recommends the establishment of a Training Charter which would lay down the VET infrastructure to which industry would be expected to comply.

With regard to employment relations, the following recommendations, to be enacted largely through government action (including legislation), were made: first, it was proposed to establish *statutory* workplace training committees structured in a similar way to health and safety committees. These committees would be responsible for drawing up an enterprise training plan and for monitoring its progress. Second, at a regional level, TECs would be retained, but membership expanded 'to more adequately reflect the communities they serve'. Membership would be open to union and local authority representatives, among others. In association with local education interests, the revised TECs would be responsible for drawing up local training plans.

Third, to help meet the needs of individual industries, the TUC also commends the establishment of supervisory bodies, Industry Training Organisations, aimed at monitoring skill needs and training provided in the appropriate sectors. At national level, a tripartite body should be set up to oversee and co-ordinate these varied training activities.

Recognising that in the past too few training programmes have been tied to the attainment of stated objectives, the TUC subsequently laid down a timetable of expected attainment up to the year 2000, by which time 70 per cent of young people should reach NVQ Level 111, equivalent to at least two 'A' level GCE passes plus five good GCSE passes.

AN ASSESSMENT OF TUC AND LABOUR PARTY PLANS

Both TUC and Labour Party would acknowledge that their plans as presently formulated are intended to signpost the general directions which vocational education and training might take rather than to specify a precise route. Generality is perhaps more marked with Labour plans, for despite their obvious appeal in broadening access, the proposals represent little more than a policy skeleton lacking in any great substance. Consequently a number of major issues have yet to be confronted. Costings for the exercise have not been specified, nor are details provided of the anticipated levels of financial contributions to be made by the various institutional participants. From the training point of view, little is said about the procedures to be implemented at work for training and development subsequent to the four-year traineeship. Though the document mentions that inputs are to be made to training policy by the involved parties, no allocation of responsibilities has been detailed. Following publication of the policy document, Labour has proposed that a legal obligation should be placed on all employers to spend a minimum of 0.5 per cent of payroll costs on training. It is doubtful whether this level of contribution would make any significant impact upon levels of training provision.

Though confirming that much needs to be done educationally, rather disappointingly, the TUC does not attempt to incorporate details of educational remedies at any great length in its substantial statement document, but concentrates on its proposals for improving the training infrastructure. Indeed, the rights specified by the TUC all concern training rather than educational entitlements, which if enacted, would not only benefit a wider proportion of the population, but could (and should) provide the base upon which subsequent training rights could be built.[1] Further, the TUC states that their network of training rights would enjoy 'legislative force' but the statement does not stipulate the ways by which this would be applied.

There are also some items included which might be difficult to enforce. The French, for example, despite their achievements in securing training expenditure in companies well in excess of the minimum legal level, have failed to achieve a high participation rate with their individual training leave provisions, and as yet little is known about the effects of this initiative. The TUC's offer of paid leave to the labour force might be difficult to implement in practice and the efforts expended could arguably be better deployed in other directions. Doubts about 'records of achievement' and training vouchers persist in the absence of strict safeguards that these devices are to benefit the long-term interests of trainees as well as to satisfy employer skill requirements.

Notwithstanding these reservations of detail, the proposals do put forward a strong conceptual case for government inclusion in training affairs. The arguments for such an approach are considered in more detail below.

THE SCOPE FOR AN INTERVENTIONIST STRATEGY IN BRITAIN

Government intervention might usefully be applied at three distinct but closely related levels, the first, in order to influence the directions and content of education; the second, to shape the deployment of labour; and the third to influence patterns of industrial and employment relations.

Throughout the 1980s, the Conservative government attempted to raise the level of employer influence and involvement in all three areas.[2] Its role in education had the intention, in the words of one critic of these policies, of reducing 'education to a species of training' (Abbs 1987).

Evidence shows that the country's interests may be better served through reversing this approach by upgrading training to the status of education. By treating initial training as a vocational branch of education with equal status to academic studies, its resourcing and direction become a natural and prime responsibility for government. A sound educational basis can then be consolidated through subsequent workplace training and development at work, guided by national interests. This educational governmental responsibility is recognised by the TUC and by the Labour Party but to a somewhat lesser extent by the CBI which considers that the:

> Government also has a central role to play. It must offer the nation a coherent vocational education and training policy, especially for young people.
> Exchequer funding must be available to provide the foundation skills which the nation requires.

(1989: 9)

Nevertheless, the CBI considers that employer involvement in education should penetrate deeper into 'work-related non-advanced education, the Technical and Vocational Education Initiative and Education Compacts' and that TECs 'will need *extensive* scope to adapt national programmes' (1989: 42, emphasis added), a perspective which with employer-dominated TECs appears to contradict the trainee-centred approach advocated by the CBI and could leave educational recipients vulnerable to the short-term or localised demands of employers who might be tempted to transfer their training requirements into State-funded but employer-driven educational programmes.

It is neither the prime intention of this book to examine in depth the potential directions which a revised education system should take, nor is this an area of expertise to which the author lays special claim. Nevertheless, an important aspect of education is its ability to feed into subsequent work-based development and for this reason broad objectives of educational reform and their implications for work-based training and for performance effectiveness should at least be considered. In particular, the following areas should be addressed:

1. There is universal acknowledgement that a significant increase in the numbers of young people pursuing full-time education after the age

of 16 is essential. A timetable for phased increases, as offered by the CBI and TUC in their reform programmes, should be laid down and the means to achieve these increases clearly stated by the government. To ensure consensus and continuity in the event of a change in administration, the support of the political opposition parties should be recruited and inputs from the main collective representations of interest (CBI, TUC, LEAs, etc.) be canvassed.

2. A three-tier system offering academic, technological and formal apprenticeship-based educational routes to age 18 should be contemplated. The technological syllabus could be developed in more rigorous form from the existing TVEI structure. The range of occupations to be covered by an apprenticeship needs to be substantially enlarged and therefore subject to review and regular appraisal by a standing committee representing both educational and industrial interests. This body, which could be modelled on the existing NCVQ in association with BTEC, should also be responsible for syllabus content and changes, for examinations and for awarding qualifications to students. Numbers gaining formal qualifications with their subsequent employment and advanced educational destinations should be published annually. The programme would be co-ordinated locally by a revised TEC.

The apprenticeship committee should act in liaison with and overlap in its membership with educational bodies responsible for academic and technological qualifications. Steps to widen the post-16 academic syllabus to prevent too early specialisation should be followed. The study of mathematics, computing and technology and associated subjects should be encouraged throughout the ability range. The establishment of a review body to examine immediate and prospective problems in the teaching profession and make recommendations for increasing the numbers of teachers, their rewards and status should be regarded as a matter of urgency.

3. Numbers of people entering higher education must be expanded toward proportions equivalent to those found in other industrialised countries and funding must be provided to resource the expansion. As there is little evidence that the existing loans system will lead to higher participation rates (see *Education Guardian*, 16 January 1990), its operation should be reviewed and alternative funding approaches considered.

4. The status of science, engineering and technology as a subject for study and a means of employment must be raised. Entrance into these occupations must be encouraged as a matter of urgency. In the longer term, this may only be possible through offering financial support in

order to expand manufacturing industry or by taking a public stake in major private concerns in order to encourage long-term growth with security. There should be study opportunities, for staff, supported by tax concessions to participating companies for upgrading existing qualifications and provisions should be made for continuing learning to keep up to date with fast moving and technological occupations whose initial study 'shelf-life' is limited.

5. Future economic growth will depend upon the performance of high technology industry, which in turn will depend upon the calibre of the people who staff the network of industry and research institutions and the resources made available to them to develop and apply technological advances. In 1981, the Japanese government initiated a ten-year programme of computer technology development aimed at increasing their share in the global information technology market from 15 per cent to at least 40 per cent. In 1984, the National Economic Development Council (NEDC) was able to report that in Britain the same industry was in decline 'due to lack of investment and skills shortages in the face of fierce international competition' which had seen Britain's market share decline to less than 5 per cent in 1984 (NATFHE 1984: 6).

If Britain is to compete in future growth areas, research and development must be allowed to flourish, and this involves government expenditure. Between 1981 and 1986, Britain was the only one of seven major OECD economies not to increase the overall share of its gross domestic product allocated to research and development, 'largely because government had not matched industry's increased expenditure' (AUT 1989: 19). The level of research spending remained at a constant 2.3 per cent of GDP through to 1989, the last year for which figures are available. In the meantime, Britain has been overtaken in proportional research expenditure by France, a country whose government has embarked upon a strategy:

> actively committed to the modernization of the French economy and society, willing to deploy the prestige, authority and resources of the state to support that modernization and eager to build an effective partnership between the public sector and private enterprise. In such a strategy research has a natural priority . . . France is investing more of its much greater national wealth in the knowledge industry, the only industry that will count in the high technology, high cost, high added value Europe of the 21st century.
>
> (*Times Higher Education Supplement*, 28 September 1990)

Until British governments are prepared to make similar investments in higher education and scientific expenditure, it will become increasingly difficult to bridge the growing gaps in the development and application of high technology and in consequence, domestic economic performance will continue to fall behind the standards set by other countries.

INDUSTRY-BASED INITIATIVES

A market-orientated approach has not succeeded in alleviating skill shortages and is unlikely to be successful in the future, for reasons which have been fully rehearsed above. There are fewer doubts about the capability of interventionist programmes to promote change. As was seen, the operation of the Industry Training Act, though undoubtedly hampered by the concerted opposition which eventually curtailed and then helped to fell this interventionist policy, did exert an overall positive effect on training provision.

The question then is not whether intervention can work: overseas experience amply demonstrates its potential effectiveness, and intervention has operated successfully, albeit on a limited scale, in Britain. The question is how can intervention best be made to work, bearing in mind the continuing attachment to voluntarism by the parties who would be most affected by an interventionist initiative and upon whom the success of the implementation would rest?

The argument to be developed rests on the simple premise that work-based training should not be a gratuity offered by employers when money is available, nor inserted by them as a short-term palliative to remedy operational impediments. It should be treated as an inherent feature of employment through its inclusion into the terms and conditions of employment or employees. For the greater part of the labour force this would require joint regulation of training through employer and employee-appointed representatives. The arguments which favour such an approach can be detailed as follows:

1. The majority of employees in Britain have their terms and conditions of employment determined through joint regulation between employer and employee representatives. Millward and Stevens report that findings from 2000 workplaces covered in the national Industrial Relations Survey show that a wide range of non-pay issues tend to be subject to joint regulation where unions are recognised (1986: tables 9.19 and 9.20). Further, a third of all (unionised and non-unionised) establishments in the survey had workplace consultative committees where 'pay and conditions were less frequently reported by managers as

the most important matter discussed', but, 'employment issues were more frequently mentioned' (1986: 309). Clearly, a framework for including training as an issue for joint discussion is available.

2. Successive British governments have followed or actively promoted industrial relations policies which are broadly consistent with supporting joint regulation, and it is an approach endorsed by the European Social Charter and its associated Action Programme (see Wedderburn 1990: 29).

3. In Chapter 1 it was argued that unions have typically adopted a positive negotiating stance to technological change when jointly involved in the change process. Most agreements which accommodate technological change, new working practices and multi-skilling include reference to training matters (Rainbird 1990: 68) and participants are becoming familiar with the contours and style of conducting adversarial but generally constructive negotiations over training. Similar non-obstructive union strategies have been observed in pensions participation and negotiation as well as in the operation of joint health and safety committees (Schuller 1986: 50). It is interesting to note that in France one of the more hardline companies, Renault, is attempting to bring about change through an enterprise-based joint agreement which rests heavily on the use of training.

4. In France, plans for workplace training are monitored through works councils and in Germany through works councils and, in industries where supervisory boards operate, by co-determination on these boards. As yet, neither of these participative approaches has taken root to any significant degree in Britain, and any government attempt to impose these participative forms would probably be met by at least suspicion and more probably resistance from at least one of the main parties affected. Employers and unions in Britain feel more secure with participative arrangements which stem from and feed into their bargaining relationships.

5. Personnel managers have amassed expertise in bargaining which they could exploit and develop to embrace training and developmental activities which they have previously tended to neglect. As part of strategic discussions with employee representatives and backed by legislation, personnel specialists would no longer be reduced to the position of passive bystander to senior management cost-cutting drives, in which training is inevitably an early casualty. Discussing training issues with workforce representatives would also encourage management to release other relevant information to union negotiators. This is not only a requirement of law where unions are recognised,[3] but also

conforms to good employment relations practice and could contribute to the development of a stable high trust relationship between the parties.

THE ROLE OF LEGISLATION

Though the training intervention will be applied through employers, unions and employees collectively, it is considered that their interactions should be backed by law. At first sight this might appear to be a departure from the stipulation that intervention can only succeed with the willing commitment of the parties, and both employers and unions have indicated a preference for freedom from direct State involvement. Nevertheless, there are good arguments for statutory backing.

First, as we have seen, voluntarism applied to an area which does not immediately impact upon the parties rarely leads to concerted action by them. This is the case presently with training, and was, until the passing of the Health and Safety at Work Act in 1974, applicable also to health and safety. There was little disagreement that steps to improve workplace health and safety were necessary but neither employers nor unions were able or prepared to take joint action until required to do so through legislation. There is also evidence from the WIRS study that appropriate enabling legislation can stimulate voluntary collective initiatives. In explaining the increase in formal procedures over dismissal and discipline, Millward and Stevens comment that: 'the continuing impact of the legislation and accompanying code of practice is apparent'. They also note that 'health and safety representation was present in an increasing proportion of workplaces' (1986: 311).

Second, the legislation will apply to non-unionised as well as unionised establishments. Relying upon voluntary means to stimulate training will risk neglecting the training needs of the 60 per cent of the workforce not currently in trade unions.

Third, legislation ensures that the requirement to allocate resources to training will be met, and that the portion so allocated will be protected if profits decline, when training expenditure would otherwise be most vulnerable. Employers (or unions) would thus not be able to 'trade off' training against immediate pay increases.

Fourth, the government's own findings in *Training in Britain* confirm the potential efficacy of a legislated programme. Over a third of training employers, including a half in manufacturing, said that legislation had served as an influence in their training activities (1989: 41–2).

So, if there are good arguments for legislating over training we need to ask what form the legislation might take. In order to bring about change at enterprise level, it is recommended that the government introduce a Training Act which requires employers to:

(a) Allocate a minimum amount of their total annual labour costs to training. In order to start to catch up with other countries, an initial level of 2 per cent should be stipulated. Non-pay training costs associated with the new apprenticeship scheme would be included within the scope of the training allocation. Additional expenditure approved by the training committee (see below) over and above the statutory minimum would be eligible for tax relief.

(b) Draw up an annual training plan including details of how it harmonises with company intentions for technological and other major enterprise changes.

(c) Present the plan to trade union representatives, where these are recognised, either for consideration as part of routine negotiations, or through a separately constituted training committee. The statutory minimum would not be negotiable, but amounts above this and the allocations of training would be open to negotiation. The employee side of the committee would be composed of elected union representatives where unions are recognised or elected members of the workforce in non-union establishments. In either case there should be parity representation between employee and managerial committee members.

There should be regular interim meetings of the committee to ensure that the agreement is being followed in practice. Enterprise committees should also be established where formal negotiations are held above establishment level, though it would be open to participants to choose the most appropriate level to undertake and resolve their training discussions. National negotiating committees involving employer associations and trade unions should also set up a joint advisory committee to monitor developments (such as technological advances) within a specific industry and refer information to workplace committees.

(d) The formally agreed arrangements for training should be signed by committee members and then submitted to a local TEC for approval. Approval would be granted if the plan meets nationally agreed criteria. One essential condition would be that, apart from under exceptional circumstances, training should invariably lead to formal qualifications. The TEC would be responsible for dispensing funds to companies whose training plans were so approved. The TEC would arrange to make regular visits to meet with training committees to ensure that plans are being conducted in accordance with the agreed plan.

(e) The TEC Board should be primarily a tripartite body with employer, union and local education authority membership, supplemented as necessary by other interests co-opted onto the Board through majority agreement. The TEC would have limited powers to amend nationally set criteria to meet local needs.

(f) Aspiring government contractors should present their agreed training plans to the government. In order to be eligible to tender for a government contract, details of the training plan, arrangements for provision and any special agreements, such as those which aim to promote greater equality, should be included. The training commitment contained in the tender document should be signed by members of the training committee or joint negotiating body, as appropriate.

CAN JOINT REGULATION WORK IN TRAINING?

The proposition that training is an appropriate area for joint regulation derives from the one major assumption that employer interests and employee interests are not necessarily co-terminous; indeed, whilst both parties usually share a general willingness to increase training as a contribution to performance, conflict may lay latent between the parties over issues such as delivery of training, its content and the occupational identity of recipients.

Support for this competing interests proposition is visible from a number of angles. We have seen, for example, that training is perceived by many, if not most, employers in Britain as a *cost of employment*. As with all costs, the prime motivation for the employer is to minimise the levels and duration of expenditure. From the point of view of employees, however, training should increase their value to the employer (and hence the price of their labour) or to other employers competing for upgraded skills of the employees. Similarly, training may increase the control over a job enjoyed by employees, as a result of raised skill levels and fewer alternative claimants for tasks which demand knowledge and skills. If trained employees take their services elsewhere, there will be the outlays foregone in the training process for the employer to consider; retraining replacement labour simply adds to the initial costs with no guarantee of subsequent benefits. For this reason of mobility, there are differences between employers and employees over the degree of generality (and hence transferability) that each party would wish to bring to training.

In tandem with treating training as a cost item, to be adjusted according to the perceived needs of employers, is the desire by employers to maintain *control* over the training process. One means of exercising control is to ensure that training provision is informal and procedures governing training remain uncodified. In support of the management control thesis, our survey showed (see Chapter 7) that employers rarely formalise or codify their training policies in association with representatives of the workforce. This behaviour would conform with patterns of industrial practice in Britain, where procedural informality has been a dominant feature of private sector employment relations for a number of years (Sisson and Brown 1983). By not entering into fixed commitments, management is able to treat labour with flexibility by withdrawing from training its staff at short notice, which, as we saw in earlier chapters, tends to happen whenever the country enters into recession or when individual employers encounter difficult trading conditions. Clearly, this variability is neither in the interests of employees, who lose training, nor in the interests of the country whose overall performance productivity becomes adversely affected.

A further perspective on the potentially conflictual nature of training is that some employees are more likely to receive training than others. The *Training in Britain* survey, for example, indicated that managers and higher status employees tend to be beneficiaries of employer training schedules rather than lesser educated and lower ranking staff (Training Agency 1989: 49). An unpublished survey covering 656 employees in a Scottish local authority helps to confirm that training and development experiences vary according to the grades of employees. Table 9.1 shows that over three-quarters of manual staff claimed never to have received any form of training. Nearly three-quarters of senior management, by contrast, had undergone off-the-job training during the *previous six months.*

An additional potential source of tension is that skill status has traditionally been reserved for men who had been selected to undertake a time-served apprenticeship. Subsequent entry without a prior apprenticeship into these occupations would be difficult for men and virtually impossible at any stage for women. Women also tend to receive restricted opportunities for training across the occupational range (Marsh 1986) and there is evidence that given the choice, employers prefer to train men rather than women (Cockburn 1985: Chapter 8).

The above points demonstrate that palpable differences exist between employer and employee interests over training. In order to ensure that these differences are resolved in a way which is acceptable

Table 9.1: Training recipients by occupation

Occupation	Off-the-job training		On-the-job training	
	Training received in past 6 months (%)	Never (%)	Training received in past 6 months (%)	Never (%)
Craft	15	40	13	44
Supervisors	11	49	13	46
Manual	2	78	3	73
Catering/Cleaning	0	93	7	71
Office/Clerical	24	42	25	30
Technical	52	35	39	39
Administration	44	21	36	31
Senior Management	72	4	35	35

Source: DOMER 1989: table 6.3.

to both sets of participants, joint regulation, which aims to secure change through compromise and consensus, should be considered as an appropriate policy option, backed by legislation to ensure that the changes in training procedure and outcomes take place along directions which are compatible with national long-term considerations.

There is substantial evidence that legislation can positively stimulate joint regulation. The range of legislative initiatives taken in the mid-1970s was aimed at raising overall levels of union involvement in workplace decision-making, whilst in specific areas such as health and safety, participative advances were also sought and achieved. As a consequence of the 1974 Health and Safety legislation, joint committees are now most commonly established in workplaces where unions are recognised (Millward and Stevens 1986: table 6.5, also p. 311).

Nevertheless, voluntary steps for union inclusion in decision-making are taken by employers, though in fact, some ostensibly voluntary initiatives in joint regulation can trace their origins either to State action or to the prospect of it. Hence, a rise in consultative processes occurred following the publication of the Bullock Report on industrial democracy (Cressey *et al.* 1981: 53–4; Poole 1986: 75–6). Likewise the 1975 Social Security and Pensions Act was largely responsible for the proliferation in pensions bargaining and joint membership of pensions committees which occurred in the years following the Act (Hyman and Schuller 1984).

Even voluntary moves not attached to or deriving from a governmental initiative can usually be traced to some wish by the employer to bring about change with regard to work or the ways in which it is performed. The state of existing political and economic conditions will help to dictate whether employers enter into (or vary) collective arrangements with unions. Hence, the patterns and depth of collective bargaining tend to fluctuate according to economic and other contextual circumstances. The potential instability of collective bargaining coverage provides a substantive justification for the support of legislation to buttress the training moves advocated above; it should provide the stability for training provision that has never previously been achieved in Britain but is now essential if permanent and progressive change is to occur.

A good example of a programme of negotiated educational and training change which is linked to company need for heightened performance is the Employee Development and Assistance Programme (EDAP) launched by the Ford Motor Company (UK) in association with its union negotiating partners. The scheme was agreed as part of the 1987 annual negotiations between the company and both salaried and manual union negotiators. The stated aim of the agreement was 'to provide opportunities for personal development and training outside working hours for all employees of the company' (minutes of the agreement, quoted in Mortimer 1990: 309), but implicit objectives were to secure improvements to the industrial relations climate by encouraging staff and manual unions to work together in association with Ford management and, essentially, to:

> assist the change in the overall organisational development climate of
> the company by delegating responsibility and authority for a signi-
> ficant programme with considerable finances to joint groups of union
> representatives and management.
>
> (Mortimer 1990: 309)

The EDAP scheme was not introduced with the intention of displacing routine task-centred training provided by the company, but both immediate and indirect organisational benefits were envisaged to stem from the programme, and these may also be associated with the sort of challenges which prompted Renault to enter into its recent training agreement (see p. 76).

The scheme works along the following lines. For the first year of the scheme the company contributed £40 for every employee, resulting (along with external contributions to the programme) in a total of £1.8

million for allocation. The company assumed a 20 per cent participation rate, providing an average distribution of £200 per employee annually to contribute to their individual development. At first glance, this amount seems comparatively modest, but it may be recalled that large companies in the survey only spent an average £111 annually for the development of each employee, whereas the EDAP allocation is offered in addition to any occupational training provided by the company. Another major factor is that the scheme is handled on a completely joint basis between unions and management. At company level, the scheme is co-ordinated by a National Joint Programme Committee involving members of the staff unions, manual unions and management with a generally supervisory brief, laying down the general procedures for the locally constituted LJPCs (Local Joint Programme Committees) to follow. The local committees meet on a fortnightly basis in order to review developments, screen applications and monitor spending. The Halewood (Liverpool) LJPC had over £250,000 for allocation to its 10,000 employees in the first year of the scheme.

Initial evaluation of the scheme is underway through external assessors, but already there are positive signs. In the first year, 30 per cent of the workforce had signed up for EDAP studies, opening up new areas for study which assist both in the development of the individual employee and, less directly perhaps, in furthering company interests through employing more confident and adaptable employees, and through creating 'shared responsibility and a non-adversarial style (which) are novel for all parties concerned and the lessons learned should reflect in improving normal working relationships on the shop-floor' (Mortimer 1990: 313).

Generally, these changes may be necessary if Ford is to compete effectively against other vehicle producers or for Ford UK to maintain its internal position in the company's European operations. According to an internal report, the main challenge facing the major car assembly plant at Dagenham is to reproduce the same standards of quality and productivity as are achieved in Ford's other European plants. The 1989 report specifies that 'the survival of this plant depends totally upon achieving improved quality, reliability of supply and productivity'. Nevertheless, positive changes had taken place with

a marked improvement in employee relations in most areas of the organisation. We have been able to achieve changes in production shifts, work allocation and levels of employment, without major conflict.

The changes have been brought about by a combination of actions ranging from a more open management style, a willingness to involve all personnel in the changes, and of course, the realisation that the future of this plant is uncertain unless significant changes are made.

(Quoted in the *Financial Times*, 26 June 1990)

The spirit of the EDAP agreement is consistent with the pursuit of performance productivity and changes in management style noted above. The agreement also recalls the comments of the Head of Training of the giant IG Metall Trade Union when discussing union inputs into training reorganisation: 'It shows that things can only happen when the unions are involved' (see p. 73). Under these circumstances, unions are not merely tolerated, but contribute actively to the decision-making process. If there are differences between management and employees, a forum is available for these differences to be aired and resolved.

Whilst the scope of the Ford programme and its enthusiastic reception from unions and employees single out EDAP for special attention it is not an isolated example. British Printing Industries, the employers' federation for the printing industry, and the National Graphical Association print union signed an agreement in 1983 which provides for company-level joint assessment of annual skill requirements, based on projections of commercial activity. Each company trainee receives an individual training agreement specifying the training to be offered. At national industry level, a Joint Training Council, with membership drawn equally from unions and employers, oversees the agreed training arrangements (TUC 1990). In the words of one commentator: 'There is no other industry in Britain today that has a set of training arrangements that are as positive and as flexible as provided under the recruitment, training and retraining agreement' (Gennard 1990: 464).

A company agreement setting up a joint management/union training committee has also been negotiated between shipbuilder Swan Hunter and five signatory unions. The intention is to provide new jointly supervised training modules to help the company and its employees to meet new skill requirements and for the company to move toward providing common terms of employment for all employees though its single status (harmonisation) programme.

In each of the cases cited above, companies in the industries concerned have undergone considerable upheaval as a result of competitive pressures and technological advances. All have experienced industrial relations difficulties in attempting to cope with these changes. If joint training programmes can be introduced into these hard pressed sectors, there seems little reason to doubt that those industries and enterprises with less abrasive employment relations traditions can successfully bring training under joint stewardship, given the favourable conditions provided by the proposed legislation.

THE POSITION OF SMALL COMPANIES

The findings presented in Chapter 7 confirm that small companies spend proportionately less on training than do larger ones. The reasons are familiar: smaller concerns face considerable constraints due to time problems, lack of awareness of training opportunities and incompatibility of generic training programmes with the specific needs of the small-firm sector. Moreover, 'their managers frequently lack the strategic management skills needed to allow their businesses to grow' (*Financial Times*, Editorial, 11 July 1990). These companies (and the staff they employ) are also most vulnerable to economic disturbances; during the 12 months to December 1990, small firm failures were running at some 1,600 a month compared with 1,000 a month a year earlier. In uncertain economic climates the imperative to train may be submerged by more pressing concerns.

Small companies were highly vociferous in their opposition to the bureaucratic laboriousness of the levy-grant system provided for in the 1964 Industry Training Act. Collectively, small independent companies do not generally welcome government interference in their affairs. On the other hand, there are complaints that governmental communication channels which small firms would wish to utilise are either poorly designed or relatively under-funded; according to one recent study, small companies would like to establish closer ties with government over issues which most concern them (MacMillan *et al.* 1990). One could assume that survival and growth would figure prominently in these concerns.

The problem, though, is to convince small firms that they would benefit from training applied to both their management and employees. Exhortation appears to have failed and, therefore, it is recommended that smaller concerns should not be exempted from the statutory requirement to train outlined above, but in order to ensure willing compliance with the legislation the arrangements should be simplified and made compatible with small firm needs.

For establishments with less than twenty-five employees it is suggested that owners or their representatives draw up the necessary annual training plan, aided if requested, by a small-company specialist attached to the appropriate TEC. The plan would then be forwarded to a specialist small-firm section of the TEC for approval. This section would receive all notifications from small firms and would help to establish and co-ordinate appropriate training facilities (such as group training, small firm MBAs, networking, assistance from large customers) on the basis of the collected training plans laid down by the companies.

As with larger organisations, approved training would require compliance with nationally established qualification standards, which would include the expanded range of apprenticeship-based occupations. TEC small-company specialists would arrange to make regular visits to small companies. Provision would be made for representatives of small-firm organisations to sit on the main board of each TEC and these representatives would also be prominent in the specialist small-firm section. There is a danger that TECs, as presently constructed, with their broad membership composed of at least two-thirds local senior management, might overlook or misinterpret the needs and views of small local companies and their employees. It is hoped that, whilst the approach outlined above is not expected to overcome all the objections of small firm owner/managers, it will at least offer a genuine forum for their expression and possible resolution. Essentially, it will also mean that small firms will increase their training and development efforts and thereby help to fulfil their growth potential.

SUMMARY

Over the past ten years, public policy has presented employers with apparently unprecedented opportunities to re-shape employment relations in pursuit of levels of performance achieved by industry in other countries. In these countries, one of the ways to increase performance productivity has been to enhance the competence of managers and workforce employed in industry through prior education and through subsequent systematic development. In Britain, competitive market conditions and the absence of government controls have together worked *against* employers taking the long-term steps required to reconstruct the skills and educational base needed by the economy. Working under short-term constraints has forced employers to seek out short-term solutions.

The consequence, shown by research findings and by the experience of chronic skill shortages persisting amidst long-standing (and now growing) unemployment, is an unstable economy increasingly ill-equipped to keep pace with its trading partners and competitors. This chapter has endeavoured to suggest means by which the diverse interests of industry, employees, unions, educational services and the State may be mobilised in order to create a feasible approach to vocational education and training in Britain.

It is appreciated that the policy options suggested above will not meet with the approval of all participants to the training and education debate; the multi-stranded nature of a pluralist society ensures a multiplicity of views. It is recognised also that resource issues must be confronted. Any investment to secure future benefit requires an initial contribution of funds. The prime responsibility for this outlay will fall upon a government which will not be able to bask in the glory of immediate benefits: hence the need for political consensus in order that long-term plans are not thwarted through change of administration, or abandoned in the face of short-term but ultimately self-defeating expediency.

Finally, it is recognised that steps to improve long-term performance through training and education cannot take place in a vacuum. Industry must receive assurances from government and support from financial interests for its future in terms of funding for investment and development. Pressures exerted upon industry for short-term performance must be relaxed. A heavy responsibility rests upon government to create the conditions for controlled consistent growth. Reliance on market forces has not and cannot provide these growth conditions.

Notes

Introduction

1 Formal training refers to the provision of generally acceptable evidence for skills attained at work. Evidence would normally be found in qualifications obtained from validating bodies such as the NCVQ etc.
2 See Hyman and Bell (1989). This study was confined to private sector companies for the following reasons. Unions in the public sector have shown little enthusiasm toward some government schemes, such as Employment Training (ET). This hostility has restricted the use of ET in the public sector. Individual private sector employers, by contrast, have more freedom to choose whether to participate in government schemes. Further, the government is locating its training policies around private sector company involvement (see Chapter 3).

2 The response of the State. Reforms of industrial relations and education

1 Moreover, as Keep has observed, in contrast to the United States and Germany, Britain suffers from a dearth of manpower planning information, which has meant that organising any educational provision for employment needs has been very much a hit and miss affair (1989: 182).

4 Training policies and practices in other countries

1 Training has been broadly classified as 'general' or 'specific', with the former offering skills readily transferable to other employers, and the latter offering no ready transfer. Economic analysts have contended that under competitive market conditions, training recipients will pay for general training, through low pay during the training period, as they benefit financially through their subsequent higher productivity and mobility. Employers are prepared to pay for specific training as they will benefit from resultant higher productivity which, due to its uniqueness, competing employers are unable to poach. Craft training is generally regarded as a form of general skill acquisition. Specific

training includes induction programmes and highly specialised new technology familiarisation schemes (see Becker 1964; Ziderman 1978).

2 Loyalty is also expressed in long working hours, low rates of absenteeism, short holidays often not taken in full, overall low rates of industrial disputes and social life which for many employees revolves around the work community and its 'citizens' (see Eccleston 1989; Hanami 1980: Japan Institute of Labour 1990: tables 32–47).

The *Japan Labour Bulletin*, March 1990, reports that 'Japanese spend more time at work than people in other industrialized nations and are criticized for being "workaholics"'. These comments were based upon the findings of an international survey which revealed that less than 20 per cent of Japanese questioned 'said that they enjoyed a true five-day working week'.

5   Training provision in Britain

1 In some cases, as with government-funded academic professional studies, recent government intervention has gone rather further than the catalytic input assumed under voluntarism. This role has been undertaken by directly influencing the expansion or contraction of courses through access to funding (e.g. by trying to close veterinary schools on grounds of over-supply of veterinary surgeons).

2 Kolb and his co-workers envisage a cycle of learning in which four main factors interact to influence the ways and efficiency with which people learn. These factors are the concrete experience undergone by the learner; observation and reflection; formation of abstract concepts and theorisation; and testing the concepts in new or different circumstances, which leads to more concrete experience, thereby maintaining the cycle and developing the learning (Kolb *et al.* 1974).

As a continuous cycle, learning need not necessarily originate with experience; any of the main stages can trigger and sustain learning through the cycle. Subsequently, this led the researchers to suggest that different individuals and occupations would emphasise specific stages of the cycle as their preferred means of learning, leading to a categorisation of dominant learning styles for different managerial and technical functions.

Mumford and Honey have attempted to further rationalise and operationalise learning styles. Trainees can then be selected for specific programmes which, by adopting their preferred style, can be expected to result in effective learning. Other subsequences of this interest are that researchers are actively investigating organisational and contextual factors which might impede or promote learning. Kolb's studies have also led to consideration of the value of experience to formal learning programmes (such as MBA) and to examine the ways in which experiences may be structured in order to gain full benefit for learners and organisation, whether at work through 'mentoring' and counselling schemes or in academic business courses (see Kenney and Reid 1988; Mumford 1985).

6 Training and the personnel function

1 Indeed, fears of higher-level involvement by employees led to the concerted resistance by employers both to the plans for worker directors contained in the Bullock Report (1977) and to the more recent European Social Charter proposals.

7 Training in practice

1 This section originates from and builds upon an article 'Training and small companies; some Scottish evidence' which appeared in the Fraser of Allander *Quarterly Economic Commentary*, Vol 15, No 4, June 1990.

8 A way forward? The market approach

1 The document was prepared by a Task Force of senior executives drawn from the business community. Findings were debated at the 1989 annual conference of the CBI which unanimously endorsed the contents. The report became CBI policy following its adoption by the CBI Council.
2 Two examples are the introduction of training vouchers on an experimental basis, and the merging of the functions of the Training Agency in Scotland with those of the Scottish Development Agency to form a new body, Scottish Enterprise (Danson *et al.* 1989).
3 For its 1990 conference, the CBI acknowledges that growth in higher education is imperative and argues that the government has a 'key role' to: 'establish principles for the funding of higher education that allow a significant expansion to take place over the next 10 years and recognise that students should contribute their support costs' (CBI National Conference 1990).

9 A way forward? Government intervention

1 It is true that the TUC states in the document that its policies for education are not included as they are set out elsewhere. But as it also states that training and education are inseparable, it seems that they should be treated as such by TUC policies. If not, there is a danger that 'vocational' education will continue to be perceived and treated as a separate and inferior branch of education.
2 At the same time the government attempted to suppress the influence of bodies such as local education authorities and especially trade unions whose actions might not be completely supportive of a market-driven economic policy. In this sense, the government did assume to itself a considerable degree of control in areas in which it previously maintained a reasonable distance, paradoxically in order to encourage the freedoms of the market over these same areas.
3 The Employment Protection Act 1975 entitles a union which is recognised by the employer for the purposes of collective bargaining to 'all such infor-

mation relating to his undertaking as in his possession, or that of an associated employer' which 'would be in accordance with good industrial relations practice' to disclose. For the difficulties faced by unions in translating this legal requirement into practice, see Dickens and Bain (1986).

References

Abbs P. (1987) 'Training spells the death of education', *Guardian*, 5 January.

Adams R. J. and Rummel C. H. (1977) 'Workers' participation in management in West Germany: Impact on the workers, the enterprise and the trade union', *Industrial Relations Journal*, Vol 8, No 1.

Ainley P. and Corney M. (1990) *Training for the Future: The Rise and Fall of the Manpower Services Commission*, London, Cassell.

Ashcroft B., Love J. and Malloy E. (1989) Entrepreneurial Activity in Scotland: The Case of Firm Formation, Final Report to the Standing Commission on the Scottish Economy, May.

Asher P. (1989) 'Equal opportunities for Black people', *Education and Training UK*, Policy Journals.

Association of University Teachers (AUT) (1989) *The Case for Increased Investment in UK Universities*, July.

Baldry C. (1985) 'Learning from Japan' *International Labour Reports*, July/August.

Ball C. (1990) *More Means Different: Widening Access to Higher Education*, Royal Society for the Encouragement of Arts, Manufacturers and Commerce, May.

Becker G. S. (1964) *Human Capital: A Theoretical and Empirical Analysis*, New York, National Bureau of Economic Research.

Bell D. W. and Hanson C. G. (1987) *Profit-Sharing and Profitability: How Profit-Sharing Promotes Business Success*, London, Kogan Page.

Benn C. and Fairley J. (1986) *Challenging the MSC*, London, Pluto.

Blaug M. (1970) *An Introduction to the Economics of Education*, Harmondsworth, Penguin.

Blyton P. (1990) 'Hitting the factory floor', *Times Higher Education Supplement*, 9 November.

Braverman H. (1974) *Labour and Monopoly Capital*, New York, Monthly Review Press.

Brewster C. and Smith C. (1990) 'Corporate strategy: A no-go area for personnel', *Personnel Management*, July.

Brewster C. J., Gill C. G. and Richbell S. (1981) 'Developing an analytical approach to IR policy', *Personnel Review*, Vol 10, No 2.

Brittan S. (1990) 'Time to cheer up a little', *Financial Times*, 31 May.

Bullock, Lord (1977) *Report of the Committee of Inquiry on Industrial Democracy*, CMND 6706, HMSO.

Casey B. (1986) 'The dual apprenticeship system and the recruitment and retention of young persons in West Germany', *British Journal of Industrial Relations*, Vol XXIV, No 1.

Cassels J. (1990) *Britain's Real Skill Shortage*, London, PSI.

CEDEFOP (1990) *Joint Opinion on Education and Training*, Special 5/90, European Centre for the Development of Vocational Training.

Chapman P. G. and Tooze M. J. (1987) *The Youth Training Scheme in the United Kingdom*, Aldershot, Avebury.

Chapman R. (1990) 'Personnel management in the 1990s', *Personnel Management*, January.

Chitty C. (1986) 'TVEI: The MSCs Trojan horse' in C. Benn and J. Fairley (eds) *Challenging the MSC*, London, Pluto.

Cockburn C. (1985) *Machinery of Dominance*, London, Pluto.

Cockburn C. (1987) *Two-Track Training: Sex Inequalities in the YTS*, Basingstoke, Macmillan.

Confederation of British Industry (CBI) (1987) *Current Management Attitudes*, London.

Confederation of British Industry (CBI) (1989) *Towards a Skills Revolution*, London.

Constable J. and McCormick R. (1987) *The Making of British Managers*, London, BIM/CBI.

Coopers and Lybrand Associates (1985) *A Challenge to Complacency: Changing Attitudes to Training*, London, MSC/NEDO.

Cressey P., Eldridge J., MacInnes J. and Norris G. (1981) *Industrial Democracy and Participation: A Scottish Survey*, Department of Employment Research Paper, No 28, November.

Crewe L. (1991) 'New technologies, employment shifts and gender divisions within the textile industry', *New Technology, Work and Employment*, Vol 6, No 1, Spring.

Dale R. (1985) 'The background and inception of the Technical and Vocational Education Initiative' in R. Dale (ed.) *Education, Training and Employment*, Oxford, Pergamon.

Daly A., Hitchens D. M. W. N. and Wagner K. (1985) 'Productivity, machinery and skills in a sample of British and German manufacturing plants' in *Productivity, Education and Training*, London NIESR (1989).

Daniel W. W. (1987) *Workplace Industrial Relations and Technical Change*, London, Frances Pinter/PSI.

Daniel W. W. and Millward N. (1983) *Workplace Industrial Relations in Britain: The DE/PSI/ESRC Survey*, Aldershot, Gower.

Danson M., Lloyd G. and Newlands D. (1989) '"Scottish Enterprise": The creation of a more effective agency or the pursuit of ideology', *Quarterly Economic Commentary*, Vol 14, No 3, Fraser of Allander Institute, University of Strathclyde, March.

Department of Education and Science (DES) (1989) *Aspects of Higher Education in the United States of America*, London, HMSO.

Dickens L. and Bain G. S. (1986) 'A duty to bargain? Union recognition and information disclosure' in R. Lewis (ed.) *Labour Law in Britain*, Oxford, Blackwell.

DOMER (Department of Organisation, Management and Employment Relations) (1989) Employee Attitudes Towards Compulsory Competitive Tendering, unpublished report, University of Strathclyde, April.

Donovan Report (1968) Royal Commission on Trade Unions and Employers Associations 1965–1968, Comnd 3623.

Dore R. P. (1985) 'Financial structures and the long-term view', *Policy Studies*, 6 (Part 1).

Dore R. P. and Sako M. (1989) *How the Japanese Learn to Work*, London, Routledge.

Eccleston B. (1989) *State and Society in Post-War Japan*, Cambridge, UK, Polity Press.

Education Guardian (1990) 16 January.

Egor Group (1990) *Training and Employment of Engineers in Europe*, Paris.

Employment Committee (1990) *Employment Training*, Employment Committee, House of Commons, Third Report, 16 May, London HMSO.

Employment for the 1990s (1988) White Paper, Com 540, December.

Employment Gazette (1989), Vol 97, No 3, March.

Estrin S. and Wadhwani S. (1986) *Will Profit-Sharing Work?*, London, Employment Institute.

European Industrial Relations Review (1990) 'Renault modernises its industrial relations policy', No 194, March.

European Industrial Relations Review (1990) 'Law on training', No 200, September.

Fairley J. (1981) 'Industrial training in Scotland' in H. Drucker and N. Drucker (eds) *Scottish Government Yearbook 1982*, Edinburgh.

Financial Times (1988) 25 August, 2 September, 16 September, 7 November, 8 December.

Financial Times (1990) 23 January, 31 January, 17 March, 22 May, 31 May, 26 June, 3 December.

Financial Times (1991) 2 January, 20 February.

Finegold D. and Soskice D. (1988) 'The failure of training in Britain: Analysis and prescription', *Oxford Review of Economic Policy*, Vol 4, No 3, Autumn.

Finn D. (1987) *Training Without Jobs*, Basingstoke, Macmillan.

Flude M. and Hammer M. (eds) (1990) *The Education Reform Act 1988*, London, Falmer.

Fogarty M. and Brooks D. (1986) *Trade Unions and British Industrial Development*, London, PSI.

Fonda N. and Hayes C. (1986) 'Is more training really necessary?', *Personnel Management*, May.

Fowler A. (1988) 'New directions in performance pay', *Personnel Management*, November.

Fox A. (1974) *Beyond Contract: Work, Power and Trust Relations*, London, Faber.

Fox A. (1985) *History and Heritage*, London, Allen & Unwin.

Fulton O. (1987) 'The Technical and Vocational Education Initiative: An assessment' in A. Harrison and J. Gretton (eds) *Education and Training UK*, Newbury, Policy Journals.

Gallagher C., Daly M. and Thomason J. (1990) 'The growth of UK companies

1985–87 and their contribution to job generation', *Employment Gazette*, Vol 98, No 2, February.

Gamble A. (1981) *Britain in Decline*, London, Macmillan.

Gapper J. (1990) 'Heavy ripples in a stagnating pond', *Financial Times*, 27 January.

Gennard J. (1990) *A History of the National Graphical Association*, London, Unwin Hyman.

Golby M. (1987) 'Vocationalism and education' in M. Holt (ed.) *Skills and Vocationalism*, Milton Keynes, Open University Press.

Gospel H. F. (ed.) (1991) *Industrial Training and Technological Innovation*, London, Routledge.

Guardian (1988) 27 June.

Guardian (1989) 25 October.

Guardian (1990) 12 January, 19 January, 22 January, 7 February, 9 February, 22 September, 14 December, 15 December.

Hakim C. (1989) 'Identifying fast grow small firms', *Employment Gazette*, January.

Hammermesh D. S. and Rees A. (1984) *The Economics of Work and Pay* (3rd edn), New York, Harper & Row.

Hanami T. (1980) *Labour Relations in Japan Today*, London, John Martin.

Handy C. (1987) 'Management training: Perk or requisite?', *Personnel Management*, May.

Handy C., Gordon C., Gow I. and Randlesome C. (1988) *Making Managers*, London, Pitman.

Helsby G. (1989) 'Central control and grassroots creativity: The paradox at the heart of TVEI' in *Education and Training UK*, Newbury, Policy Journals.

Hinchcliffe P. (1990) 'Imagination is more important than knowledge', *Textile Horizons*, February.

Hussey D. (1988) *Management Training and Corporate Strategy*, Oxford, Pergamon.

Hyman J. and Bell K. R. (1989) 'A training revolution? The experience of Scotland', Discussion Paper No 1, University of Strathclyde.

Hyman J. and Boyle S. (1989) 'Training and development in the private sector in Scotland' *Quarterly Economic Commentary*, Vol 14, No 3, Fraser of Allander Institute, University of Strathclyde, March.

Hyman J. and Schuller T. (1984) 'Occupational pension schemes and collective bargaining', *British Journal of Industrial Relations*, Vol 22, No 3.

Hyman R. (1989) *Strikes* (4th edn), Basingstoke, Macmillan.

Incomes Data Services (1980) *Industrial Training Boards*, Study No 224, August.

Incomes Data Services (1990) *Profit Sharing and Share Options*, Study No 468, October.

Ingram P. and Lindop E. (1990) 'Can unions and productivity ever be compatible?', *Personnel Management*, July.

Institute of Manpower Studies (IMS) (1984) *Competence and Competition*, London, MSC/NEDO.

Institute of Personnel Management (IPM) (1986) *Profit-Related Pay: A Consultative Document*, London, IPM.

Jameson I. (1985) 'Corporate hegemony or pedagogic liberation: the schools –

industry movement in England and Wales' in R. Dale (ed.) *Education, Training and Employment*, Oxford, Pergamon.

Japan Institute of Labour (1986) *Problems of Working Women*, Tokyo, Japan Institute of Labour.

Japan Institute of Labour (1990) *Japanese Working Life Profile*, Tokyo, Japan Institute of Labour.

Japan Labour Bulletin (1990) 'Working conditions and the labour market', Vol 29, No 3, March.

Jarvis V. and Prais S. J. (1989) ' Two nations of shopkeepers: Training for retailing in France and Britain', *National Institute Economic Review*, No 128, May.

Jones I. (1986) 'Apprenticeship training in British manufacturing establishments: Some new evidence' *British Journal of Industrial Relations*, Vol 24, No 3, November.

Jones I. (1988) 'An evaluation of YTS' *Oxford Review of Economic Policy*, Vol 4, No 3, Autumn.

Keep E. (1989) 'A training scandal' in K. Sisson (ed.) *Personnel Management in Britain*, Oxford, Blackwell.

Kellner P. (1990) 'Myopic market will not rescue a city in decline', *Independent*, 13 July.

Kelly J. (1988) *Trade Unions and Socialist Politics*, London, Verso.

Kenney J. and Reid M. (1988) *Training Interventions* (2nd edn), London, IPM.

Kinnie N. and Lowe D. (1990) 'Performance-related pay on the shopfloor' *Personnel Management*, November.

Kochan T., Katz H. and Mckersie R. B. (1986) *The Transformation of American Industrial Relations*, New York, Basic.

Kogan M. (1985) 'Education policy and values' in I. McNay and J. Ozga (eds) *Policy Making in Education*, Oxford, Pergamon.

Kolb D. A., Rubin I. M. and McIntyre J. M. (1974) *Organisational Psychology – an Experiential Approach*, Englewood Cliffs, NJ, Prentice Hall.

Labour Policy Document (1990) 'Investing in Britain's Future', London.

Labour Research (1988), 'UK training at the bottom of the class', Vol 77, No 1, January.

Labour Research (April 1990) 'Education for the privileged few', Vol 79, No 4.

Labour Research (September 1990) 'Low marks for the national curriculum', Vol 79, No 9.

Labour Research Dept (1990) *Bargaining Report (Training)*, January.

Lane C. (1989) *Management and Labour in Europe*, Aldershot, Edward Elgar.

Lane C. (1990) 'Vocational training, employment relations and new production concepts in Germany: Some lessons for Britain', *Industrial Relations Journal*, Vol 21, No 4, Winter.

Lee D., Marsden D., Rickman P. and Duncombe J. (1990) *Scheming for Youth*, Milton Keynes, Open University Press.

Lees D. and Chiplin R. (1970) 'The economics of industrial training', *Lloyds Bank Review*, April.

Livy B. (1988) *Corporate Personnel Management*, London, Pitman.

Long P. (1986) *Performance Appraisal Revisited*, London, IPM.

MacInnes J. (1987) *Thatcherism at Work*, Milton Keynes, Open University Press.

MacKay L. and Torrington D. (1986) *The Changing Nature of Personnel Management*, London, IPM.

McLeish H. (1990) 'Who pays for skills?', Labour Market Briefing 3, London, House of Commons.

McLoughlin I. and Clark J. (1988) *Technological Change at Work*, Milton Keynes, Open University Press.

MacMillan K., Curran J. and Downing S. (1990) 'Government consultation with small business owners', *International Small Business Journal*, Vol 8, No 4.

Mangham I. and Silver M. S. (1986) *Management Training: Context and Practice*, London, ESRC.

MSC (1981) 'A New Training Initiative: A Consultative Document', London.

Mant A. (1969) *The Experienced Manager: A Major Resource*, London, BIM.

Marginson P. and Sisson K. (1988) 'The management of employees' in P. Marginson *et al. Beyond the Workplace*, Oxford, Blackwell.

Marginson P., Edwards P. K., Martin R., Purcell J. and Sisson K. (1988) *Beyond the Workplace: Managing Industrial Relations in the Multi-establishment Enterprise*, Oxford, Blackwell.

Marsden D. and Ryan P. (1989) 'Employment and training of young people' in *Education and Training UK*, Newbury, Policy Journals.

Marsh S. (1986) 'Women and the MSC' in C. Benn and J. Fairley (eds) *Challenging the MSC*, London, Pluto.

Mayes D. G. and Moir C. B. (1989) 'Small firms in the UK economy', *Royal Bank of Scotland Review*, December.

Millward N. and Stevens M. (1986) *British Workplace Industrial Relations 1980–1984*, Aldershot, Gower.

Mortimer K. (1990) 'EDAP at Ford: A research note', *Industrial Relations Journal* Vol 21, No 4, Winter.

Mumford A. (1985) 'What's new in management development', *Personnel Management*, May.

Mumford A. (1987) 'Learning styles and learning', *Personnel Review*, Vol 6, No 3.

National Association of Teachers in Further and Higher Education (NATFHE) (1984) *Britain's Future: The Economy and Higher Education*, November.

NATFHE Journal (1989) 'Independent governors appointed to Higher Education Corporation Boards', Summer.

National Economic Development Council (NEDC) (1963) *Conditions Favourable to Foster Growth*, London, HMSO.

NIESR (1989) *Productivity, Education and Training*, London, December.

Nichols T. (1986) *The British Worker Question*, London, RKP.

Niven M. (1967) *Personnel Management 1913–1963*, London, IPM.

Oechslin J. (1987) 'Training and the business world: The French experience', *International Labour Review*, Vol 126, No 6, November/December.

Oliver N. and Wilkinson B. (1989) 'Japanese management techniques and personnel and industrial relations practice in Britain: Evidence and implications', *British Journal of Industrial Relations*, Vol 27, No 1, March.

Owen Smith E. (1971) *Productivity Bargaining*, London, Pan.

Pearson P. (1985) *Twilight Robbery: Trade Unions and Low Paid Workers*, London, Pluto.

Pearson R., Pike G., Gordon A. and Wecgman C. (1989) 'How many graduates in the twenty-first century', Summarised in IMS Report, No 177.

Personnel Management (1988) Letter to the editor, May.

Peters T. J. and Waterman R. H. (1982) *In Search of Excellence*, New York, Harper & Row.

Poole M. (1986) *Towards a New Industrial Democracy*, London, Routledge.

Prais S. J. (1987) 'Evaluating for productivity: Comparisons of Japanese and English schooling and vocational preparation' in *Productivity, Education and Training*, London, NIESR (1989).

Prais S. J. (1989) 'Qualified manpower in engineering' in *Productivity, Education and Training*, London, NIESR.

Prais S. J. and Steedman H. (1986) 'Vocational training in France and Britain: The building trades' in *Productivity, Education and Training*, London, NIESR (1989).

Prais S. J. and Wagner K. (1985) 'Schooling standards in England and Germany: Some summary comparisons bearing on economic performance' in *Productivity, Education and Training*, London, NIESR (1989).

Prais S. J., Jarvis V. and Wagner K. (1989) 'Productivity and vocational skills in services in Britain and Germany: Hotels' in *Productivity, Education and Training*, London, NIESR.

Pratt K. J. and Bennett S. G. (1985) *Elements of Personnel Management* (2nd edn), Wokingham, Van Nostrand Reinhold.

Price Waterhouse/Cranfield (1990) Project on International Strategic HRM, Report.

Purcell J. (1987) 'Mapping management styles in employee relations', *Journal of Management Studies*, Vol 24, No 5.

Purcell J. and Sisson K. (1983) 'Strategies and practice in the management of industrial relations' in G. S. Bain (ed.) *Industrial Relations in Britain*, Oxford, Blackwell.

Rainbird H. (1990) *Training Matters*, Oxford, Blackwell.

Rainnie A. (1989) *Industrial Relations in Small Firms*, London, Routledge.

Randell P. (1989) 'Employee appraisal' in K. Sisson (ed.) *Personnel Management in Britain*, Oxford, Blackwell.

Ranson S. (1990) 'From 1944 to 1988: Education, Citizenship and Democracy' in M. Flude and M. Hammer (eds) *The Education Reform Act 1988*, London, Falmer.

Rose R. (1990) 'Prospective evaluation through comparative analysis: Youth training in a time-space perspective', *Studies in Public Policy*, No 182, University of Strathclyde.

Royal Borough of Windsor and Maidenhead (1986) *Performance Management*, Management Services Unit.

Sadler P. (1989) 'Management development' in K. Sisson (ed.) *Personnel Management in Britain*, Oxford, Blackwell.

Sako M. and Dore R. (1988) 'Teaching or testing: The role of the State in Japan', *Oxford Review of Economic Policy*, Vol 4, No 3.

Schuller T. (1986) *Age, Capital and Democracy*, Aldershot, Gower.

Scottish Business Insider (March 1990) 'Enterprise culture in Scotland', Vol 7, No 3.

Scottish Business Insider (May 1990) 'Business lobby exercises its new enterprise muscle', Vol 7, No 5.

Scottish Education Department (1986) *Education and Training for Small Business*.

Sheldrake J. and Vickerstaffe S. (1987) *The History of Industrial Training in Britain*, Aldershot, Avebury.

Short C. (1986) 'The MSC and special measures for unemployment' in C. Benn and J. Fairley (eds) *Challenging the MSC*, London, Pluto.

Simon B. (1980) 'Education and the right offensive', in B. Simon *Does Education Matter?*, London, Lawrence & Wishart, pp. 197–216 (1985).

Simon B. (1988) *Bending the Rules: The Baker 'Reform' of Education*, London, Lawrence & Wishart.

Sisson K. (ed.) (1989) *Personnel Management in Britain*, Oxford, Blackwell.

Sisson K. and Brown W. (1983) 'Industrial relations in the private sector: Donovan revisited' in G. S. Bain (ed.) *Industrial Relations in Britain*, Oxford, Blackwell.

Standing Commission on the Scottish Economy (1989) Final Report, November.

Steedman H. (1987) 'Vocational training in France and Britain: Office work', *National Institute Economic Review*, No 120, May.

Steedman H. (1988) 'Vocational training in France and Britain: Mechanical and electrical craftsmen', *National Institute Economic Review*, No 126, November.

Steedman H. and Wagner K. (1987) 'A second look at productivity, machinery and skills in Britain and Germany' in *Productivity, Education and Training*, London, NIESR (1989).

Steedman H. and Wagner K. (1989) 'Productivity, machinery and skills: Clothing manufacturing in Britain and Germany' in *Productivity, Education and Training*, London, NIESR.

Storey J. (1989) 'Introduction: from personnel management to human resource management' in J. Storey (ed.) *New Perspectives on Human Resource Management*, London, Routledge.

Tenne R. (1987) 'TVEI students – Three years on' *Employment Gazette*, October.

Thurley K. (1990) 'Towards a European approach to personnel management', *Personnel Management*, September.

Times Higher Education Supplement (1988) 15 April.

Times Higher Education Supplement (1990), 2 March, 6 April, 25 May, 29 May, 28 September.

Trades Union Congress (TUC) (1989) *Skills 2000*, London, TUC.

Trades Union Congress (TUC) (1990) *TUC Guidance: Joint Action Over Training*, London, TUC, August.

Training Agency (1988) *YTS: Going for Gold: An Employers' Guide*, London, HMSO.

Training Agency (1989) *Training in Britain* (main report), London, HMSO.

Training Statistics (1990) Employment Department, London, HMSO.

Turok I. and Richardson P. (1989) 'Supporting the start-up and growth of small firms', *Strathclyde Papers on Planning*, University of Strathclyde.

Tyson S. and Fell A. (1986) *Evaluating the Personnel Function*, London, Hutchinson.

Unwin L. (1990) 'Learning to live under water: The 1988 Education Reform Act and its implications for further and adult education' in M. Flude and M. Hammer (eds) *The Education Reform Act 1988*, London, Falmer.

Watts A. G. (1985) 'Education and employment' in R. Dale (ed.) *Education, Training and Employment*, Oxford, Pergamon.

Webster J. (1990) *Office Automation*, New York, Harvester Wheatsheaf.

Wedderburn Lord (1990) *The Social Charter, European Company and Employment Rights*, London, Institute of Employment Rights.

White M. (1988) 'Educational policy and economic goals', *Oxford Review of Economic Policy*, Vol 4, No 3, Autumn.

Wickens P. (1987) *The Road to Nissan*, London, Macmillan.

Williams G. (1990) 'Higher education' in M. Flude and M. Hammer (eds) *The Education Reform Act 1988*, London, Falmer.

Woodhall M. (1974) 'Investment in industrial training: An assessment of the Effects of the Industrial Training Act on the volume and costs of training', *British Journal of Industrial Relations*, Vol 12, No 1.

Ziderman A. (1978) *Manpower Training Theory and Policy*, London, Macmillan.

Index

Printed in the United States
by Baker & Taylor Publisher Services